PEACE
OF MIND
in unique verses

I0125767

Hari Datt Sharma

V&S PUBLISHERS

Published by:

V&S PUBLISHERS

F-2/16, Ansari Road, Daryaganj, New Delhi-110002
☎ 011-23240026, 011-23240027 • *Fax:* 011-23240028
Email: info@vspublishers.com • *Website:* www.vspublishers.com

Regional Office : Hyderabad

5-1-707/1, Brij Bhawan (Beside Central Bank of India Lane)
Bank Street, Koti, Hyderabad - 500 095
☎ 040-24737290
E-mail: vspublishershyd@gmail.com

Branch Office : Mumbai

Godown # 34 at The Model Co-Operative Housing, Society Ltd.,
"Sahakar Niwas", Ground Floor, Next to Sobo Central, Mumbai - 400 034
☎ 022-23510736
E-mail vspublishersmum@gmail.com

Follow us on: 🇹 🇫 in

All books available at **www.vspublishers.com**

© **Copyright:** V&S PUBLISHERS
ISBN 978-93-813844-3-5
Edition 2015

Printed at : Param Offseters Okhla New Delhi-110020

Contents

A Message from the Author

The purpose of this book is to restate and glorify a lot of ancient and basic truths about peace of mind and make you do something about applying them. I have written this book mainly in "Elated Prose Style" to help you enjoy it like poetry as well as prose. You didn't pick up this book to know how it was written. You are looking for action. So, please read a few pages carefully and if by that time you don't feel that you are acquiring a new power and a new inspiration to change your lifestyle then toss this book away. It is not good for you.

Peace of mind is the biggest problem facing mankind. Most of the religious books are based on this presumption. Hurry and worry, stress and strain are the modern enemies of peace. These must have to be subdued to protect oneself from diseases like Heart Attack, High BP, Diabetes, Ulcer, and Cancer etc. People are dying like flies due to these diseases.

Read each page rapidly at first to get a bird's-eye view of it. But if you are determined to attain peace of mind, then go back and re-read each page thoroughly. Stop frequently in your reading to think over what you are reading. Try to understand each idea. That kind of reading will aid you far more than racing ahead like a hound chasing a fox. After reading, review every page in your mind after closing your eyes.

Whatever you have read in this book, try to find out, how it can be applied in real life, otherwise you will forget it quickly. Only knowledge that is used sticks in our mind.

I am indebted to all those authors whose books inspired me and enabled me to write this book. My special gratitudes are to Dale Carnegie and Sweat Morden whose books encouraged me and prepared my mind to move towards peace of mind. I am also very thankful to His Holiness Late Swami Shivananda Ji and many other authors whose writings moved me towards peace of mind. I am not a learned man. My knowledge of English language is limited. This book is the end product of my deep studies.

I wish all of you peace of mind.

Hari Datt Sharma
Organiser
Peace of Mind Mission.

PEACE OF MIND

What is peace of mind? Is it possible to attain peace of mind? These questions often baffle many people, who have no clear conception of peace of mind. Peace of mind does not mean soothing the mind. It does not mean escape into a dream world. It means more effective participation in a real world. It does not mean innocuous lulling but dynamic stimulation of creative activity. Peace of mind greatly increases our intellectual power. It enables us to think rationally and in a better way. An excited mind can not produce rational concept or orderly thoughts. The mind is efficient only when it is cool and not hot. When our mind is heated, emotions control our judgement which proves costly in the long run. Power of the mind comes from the quietness. Nothing is as precious as peace of mind. Peace of mind is the peaceful base upon which we erect a good deal of life dynamic. Money can buy many things but not peace of mind. Nothing can bring you peace but yourself. To have peace of mind one has to discipline oneself never to get mad or resentful. It is very important to learn emotional management.

Most of the religious books emphasize to keep under control vices like lust, anger, greed, hatred, envy, jealousy and ill will etc., which are the main enemies of peace of mind. In the Gita Lord Krishna says—

> *Lust, anger and greed are the triple gates of the hell,*
> *These take the person towards the hell.*

Hurry, worry, stress and strain are the modern enemies. These enemies destroy peace of mind and produce diseases in the body. Heart troubles, ulcer, nervous breakdown like maladies are caused by these enemies of peace.

Many psychosomatic diseases like insomnia, constant fatigue, impotency, headache, indigestion etc., are caused due to unpeace of mind.

There is a right and a wrong way to do everything. There is also a right and a wrong way to live life. Living is also a science based on definite laws of nature. Those who do not cooperate with laws of nature, life goes badly. When you learn those laws and live within them, your life will be wonderful.

A person who has self control, has strength to see situations clearly. Judge them for what they are. It depends upon the attitude of your mind. Negative attitude disturbs and positive attitude provides peace to the mind.

Little things in life drive people to the edge of insanity and cause many troubles and headache. Trivialities are at the bottom of most of the marital unhappiness. Domestic wrangling, an insulting remark, a disparaging word, a rude action, false display of wealth, false display of boldness are the little things that lead to assault and murders. The small man flies into rage over the slightest criticism, but the wise man is always eager to learn from those who have censured him and reproved him.

Sharing of happiness brings happiness when the sharing is voluntary, with no other object than to give. When we try to please others, we stop thinking of ourselves. This is the very thing that protects us from worry, fear and melancholia. Serving the people without any motive makes them beam with pleasure. According to the Gita—

"With ill will and egoism, you can't be a true devotee,
Compassion is the main sign of a true devotee.
People of doubting nature can't get happiness,
Only faith and wisdom can provide happiness."

Those who do not know how to relax are slow poisoning their body. You must know how to relax your body to avoid fatigue of body and mind.

But peace of mind which you hunt outside is within you. All the worries and miseries are the creations of your mind. By changing your attitude you can easily change them.

Wealth, beauty, name, fame, prosperity and power all fail to satisfy man's inner craving. As a last resort he turns his attention within and finds there the fountain of happiness. Everybody likes peace.

1. Why to Read This Book

You would like to read this book again and again,
As it can alleviate many inner pains.
Worry, stress and strain are eating up our lives,
Heart-attack, ulcer and cancer are destroying many lives.

Many people are suffering from psychosomatic diseases,
Many are suffering from strange mental diseases.
Many diseases are caused due to un-peace of mind,
Enemies of peace always disturb the mind.

If you want to keep away all these maladies,
Peace is the only answer to get rid of these maladies.
Money can buy many things but not peace of mind,
By buying this book you can attain peace of mind.

This whole book is written in simple verses,
As mind enjoys a strange bliss while reading verses.
This book may change your outlook towards life,
Will encourage you to move towards a peaceful life.

Many striking thoughts are given in these pages,
Which were said by the holy sages.
Some may find it a thought provoking book,
As food for thought is served in this book.

It can protect you from drugs and A I D S,
As to keep mental balance you won't need dope aid.

2. Why I Write on Peace of Mind

You would like to know why I write on peace of mind?
How Peace of Mind Mission can help to attain peace of mind?
My answer is very simple and straight,
Some time tested recipes I want to state.

Life is very miserable and troublesome these days,
We have to face tension & financial troubles these days.
It has become difficult to keep pace with life,
All are feeling helpless may be a husband or a wife.

Hurry & worry, Stress and strain are giving us troubles,
And are causing cardiac, gastric and respiratory troubles.
Anxiety is producing signs of many diseases,
Heart attack, diabetes and stomach pain like diseases.

People are feeling helpless and dying like flies,
These are destroying many valuable lives.
Main cause of all these maladies is un-peace of mind.
Enemies of peace are disturbing the mind.

Most of the diseases are only psychosomatic,
Peace of mind is the tool of remedy and pragmatic.
If you want to get rid of all these maladies,
Peace of mind is the answer to fight these maladies.

Money can buy many things but not peace of mind,
That is why I dare to write on peace of mind.
I am a humble volunteer of Peace of Mind Mission,
To help you to attain peace is my sole mission.

3. Prelude to Peace of Mind

This book may guide you to attain peace of mind,
But it is only you who yourself can find.
None can physically help you to attain peace of mind,
As it solely depends upon your own inner mind.

Stress, strain and worry are the main problems these days,
Heart attack is the biggest killer in these days.
Peace of mind does not mean soothing state of mind,
But to provide a great source of energy to the mind.

It is not an escape into a dream world,
But effective participation in a real world.
It is not like innocuous lulling of a person,
But to make a dynamic and stimulating person.

It greatly increases intellectual power of mind,
A cool mind is more efficient than a hot mind.
In a hot mind emotions control the judgement,
In a cool mind moral laws control the judgement.

It can also remove sense of guilt from the mind,
Only then peace can enter and stay in the mind.
I am not telling anything new, you already did not know,
Many golden rules to get peace of mind, you also know.

Let me point out towards your ignorance and inaction,
And to restate a few basic truths to take some action.
All my recipes are time tested to attain peace of mind,
If you pick even a few, you will notice change in your mind.

My aim is to lead you towards peace of mind,
Because money can buy many things but not peace of mind.
Happiness is very rare in human life,
Money or power can't buy happiness in life.

Many philosophies of holy men prepare us to face death happily,
I want to prepare your mind to lead life happily.

4. Lust is a Big Hindrance

Lust is very common in mankind,
People have lust of many kinds.
Some have lust for welath, some for gold,
Some have lust for power, some for money to hold.

In a limit lust is a must for mankind,
After limit it often disturbs the mind.
Lust for sex keeps irritating the mind,
Makes it difficult to have peace of mind.

Lust for sex had already rolled many in the dust,
It would still roll many more in the dust.
Lust is a big hindrance to attain peace of mind,
Many take dope and wine to have peace of mind.

Lust hinders to transmute sex as a constructive force,
And dissipates creative forces of mind as a destructive force.
Lust is also known a gate to hell,
You must understand it very very well.

5. Why Lost Peace of Mind

O dear fellow, you have lost peace of mind,
Lost peace of mind, you have lost peace of mind.

You have a house and a beautiful wife,
You have many luxuries of life.
You have a telephone, T.V. and a car,
In your circle known as a star.
Then why have you lost your peace of mind?

Your children are studying in good schools,
You are a member of clubs and pools.
Have good sources of entertainment,
Now nothing is difficult for your attainment.
Then why have you lost your peace of mind?

Comforts are at your beck and call,
Servants are at your beck and call.
You can enjoy many kinds of foods,
Can drink whisky to come in mood.
Then why have you lost your peace of mind?

Many good doctors are on your roll,
Many good nurses are on your roll.
You can buy comforts of many kinds,
For pursuit of pleasure you never mind.
Then why have you lost your peace of mind?

6. Importance of Peace of Mind

I am not a gambler, I know gambling is bad,
Ultimately it makes every gambler sad,
Even then I want to have a bet with you,
Because I am sure, I will win and not you.

You have just to name only one person in the whole world,
Kindly listen carefully to all my words.
Can you name any person living with hate, jealousy and anger,
But his BP is normal and high no longer?

Can you name any rich man living with avarice and greed,
And claims, he has peace of mind indeed?
Can you name any person living a dishonest life,
But has no symptoms of heart attack, diabetes or ulcer like?

Can you name any person living a long and healthy life,
But not leading a simple and honest life?
I am sure you can't name any and will lose this bet,
Because there is a simple secret that none should forget.

Peace of mind is a rare gift for mankind,
To save them from maladies of many kinds.
Un-peace of mind causes many psychosomatic diseases,
Heart attack, diabetes, ulcer and many other diseases.

These may be easily cured with peace of mind,
Medicines provide only a temporary relief to body and mind.
Try to adopt good virtues in your life,
You will feel definite changes in your life.

You will start enjoying, what our holymen so far enjoyed,
Only peace of mind can provide you the secret of real joy.

7. Inner Enemies of Peace

If you want peaceful life, then always keep in mind,
You have to defeat inner enemies of many kinds.
Fear is the most strange enemy in our mind,
Which denies power of reasonable thinking of all kinds.

Greed is a unique enemy of the man,
It encourages selfishness in every man.
Evil partner of selfishness is the intolerance,
Which closes the mind to conceal facts of importance.

Egotism is also the enemy of the man,
It increases self love but decreases respect for other man.
Lust is always ready to roll every person in the dust,
By dissipating creative forces of mind into lust.

Anger is an insanity, always prevents right thinking,
When anybody is with rage, brain stops right thinking.
Hatred often poisons our mind and twists our thinking,
When we hate someone, impossible right thinking.

Deceit always deceives the deceiver, always keep in mind,
After providing temporary relief, it disturbs our mind.
Falsehood often weakens our spirit very low,
A liar spiritually hangs oneself and cannot bow.

Hypochondria prevents us to attain good health,
Always worrying about health, can't produce a good health.
Those who are able to overpower these enemies can e njoy peace of mind,
Those who are overpowered by them live with a disturbed mind.

8. Our Most Dangerous Enemy

Do you know any word beginning with 'A',
It does not spare anybody come what may.
It can make even a genius insane for a short time,
Very difficult to escape from its net for a long time.

It is most dangerous enemy of our heart,
Makes the people repent afterwards on their part.
Can cause disharmony in a happy family life,
Both repent afterwards may be the husband or wife.

Rage is its real brother but parents are not known,
How to escape from its net is also not known.
That word is anger which can destroy a happy family life,
A person living with rage can't enjoy a happy life.

An angry person can't judge what is wrong and what is right,
Because anger shuts off the mind making it difficult to think right.
Many situations excite us to become angry,
Try to control yourself, not to become angry.

Religious books call it a gate to hell,
Indian sages know it's harms very very well.
Wrong decisions take their origin in the fit of anger,
Egoism is also the cause of the anger.

Many diseases grow their roots in the state of anger,
Heart and nervous disorders are also caused due to anger.
Even one fit of anger can shatter the whole nervous system,
It takes many days to restore that damaged nervous system.

Try to control your anger if you want peace of mind,
Anger is the main hindrance in attaining peace of mind.

9. Who is More Poisonous than a Snake

Do you know a four letter word more poisonous than a snake,
Which gives only a momentary pleasure just like a cake.
That word is a part and parcel of our life,
None can escape from it neither husband nor wife.

*That word is **hate**—a strange enemy of mankind,*
After providing momentary pleasure damages heart and mind.
We lose our sleep due to that hate,
Our BP is increased due to that hate.

We lose health and happiness due to that hate,
Tension is increased due to that hate.
We gain nothing due to that hate,
Except tension and worry due to that hate.

Hate never hurts the person, whom we hate,
But the hater hurts his own nervous system due to that hate.
Symptoms of heart attack and stomach ulcer start recurring in life,
What is the use of that momentary pleasure that can damage our life.

Why not stop hating to avoid many maladies in life,
It will surely help you to live a happy life.
Avoid hate and feel a strange change in mind,
Which may prove a spring-board to attain peace of mind.

When we hate somebody and wish him any harm,
We harm only ourselves without doing him any harm.
We spoil our emotional happiness and peace of mind,
Feel a strange disturbance in heart and mind.

When we pray for the health and happiness of others,
We do good to ourselves rather than to others.

10. A Snake in the Grass

Do you know a five letter word, giving a strange satisfaction,
But from holy men it always gets rebuke and rejection.
For common people it is a snake in the grass,
Even then it is very darling of the mass.

*That simple word is called **greed**,*
Many paople think it a friend in need.
It encourages rich people to become even more rich,
Due to their avarice they can't tolerate any hitch.

It is the mother of covetousness causing mental strain,
It is also a cause of our heart pain.
Contentment is the worst enemy of the greed,
It is now your choice what you need.

Man filled with greed and avarice can't find peace of mind,
Contentment is very helpful to attain peace of mind.
A greedy person always violates rights of others,
In his greed won't spare even his own brothers.

Greed is a big hindrance to attain peace of mind,
Shed away your covetousness if you want peace of mind.
When greed overtakes the human mind,
It overshadows the good qualities of all kinds.

11. It is like a King Cobra Whose Poison Never Fails

Suspicion is like a king cobra whose poison never fails,
People suffering from suspicion can never hail.
It can wreck a happy life in a strange way,
Its seeds are sown in our mind by someone in anyway.

We let those seeds grow by rationalizing our own belief,
Never try to be reasonable to find some relief.
It breaks off friendship and many good relations,
Suspicion is the worst enemy of human relations.

No medicine can remove suspicion from our mind,
Wise thinking can only help a suspicious mind.
Suspicion can very easily enter in our mind,
But it is not easy to drive it away from the mind.

No doctor in the world can drive away our suspicion,
Only wise thinking can relieve us from our suspicion.
Clever and mean people use it as a weapon,
To wreck any happy life, they use this weapon.

Suspicion can separate a beloved from a lover,
It can easily separate a brother from a brother.
Suspicion can separate a husband from a wife,
It can easily wreck any human life.

Even an animal attacks due to suspicion,
It is very difficult to get rid of suspicion.
Suspicion is the most dangerous poison in the world,
It can spoil any life in the whole world.

12. Two Evil Sisters

Do you know the names of two sisters playing identical part,
One induces the mind while other induces the heart.
Mind and heart seem to like them,
As they provide a false satisfaction to them.

*If you don't know, then I tell, **Envy and Jealousy** are their*
*   names,*
Both of them have very notorious fame.
In normal condition these are part and parcel of life,
To encourage the person to make a progress in life.

But in abnormal condition they disturb the mind,
And become an enemy of peace of mind.
Envy encourages discontentment at the good fortune of others,
Jealousy encourages resentmet at the fortune of others.

They produce anger and hate in our mind,
And greatly upset our heart and mind.
Both sow the seeds of many heart troubles,
Which gradually develop into major heart troubles.

Some people can conceal all their envy,
Some can not conceal even small envy.
Some can't behave normally due to their envy,
Start saying unkind things out of their envy.

If you won't check them, you have no peace of mind,
Both are the hidden enemies of heart and mind.

13. Worst Enemy of Mankind

Do you know who is the worst enemy of mankind,
And encourages superstition of many kinds.
People hold wrong beliefs due to that enemy,
They worship many things due to that enemy.

*That enemy is **fear** causing sufferings to mankind,*
Even war breaks out when fear enters into any nation's mind.
Normal fear is a healthy sign of human life,
Abnormal fear is destructive and harmful for life.

Fear causes worry and worry causes tension,
And harms us in many ways, which I will mention.
Most of the fears are imaginary, always keep in mind,
Why not try to kick them out from your mind.

Fill your mind with boldness to defeat your fear,
You will surely find decline in your fear.
Diligently do all those things you fear the most,
It will help you to remove your fear utmost.

Parents unconsciously project their own fears in children's mind,
Who very quickly pick them up in their mind.
Never cultivate any fear in children's life,
It may keep them upset in future life.

Your fears may also have their roots in your childhood life,
Or it may owe its existence to any old memory of life.
Try to find the real cause of your fear,
Then stand up and kill at once that imaginary fear.

A long held fear pattern can't be easily changed,
But it is not impossible if you want them to change.
Our mind has very strange and peculiar quality,
It transmutes fear into a reality.

Never feel afraid of the coming events,
Let the God's will prevail in future events.

14. A Golden Rule

Do as you wish to be done by,
Is the golden rule of the wise.
Good words always produce good result,
Bad produce acrimony as a result.

Good and bad both reach straight in the ears,
Both produce different results when one hears.
Good thoughts, good words and good deeds,
Is the main teachings of all the religions indeed.

15. From *Ishawasya Upanishad**

Though I am sinful, yet there is no difference in me and Him
        (God)
I am He, and a part of Him.
This body is a covering over the essential me,
If one can pierce through the body can catch a glimpse of Thee.

---

* "Teaching of Lord" :— When we refer *"the Upanishd"* we mean those original
  ones which form part of the *Veda*.

16. Revengefulness is Very Common

Revengefulness is a common trait found in mankind,
It is found throughout the world in the same kind.
A mighty person may take its revenge at the very moment,
A weak person may await for an appropriate moment.

Revenge increases enmity without end in sight,
As a chain reaction both the sides fight.
It provides only a momentary satisfaction,
But the vital parts of the body show strange reaction.

I want to draw your attention towards another aspect,
Which requires your full attention and you can't reject.
Revengefulness strangely disturbs our mind,
And causes psychosomatic diseases of many kind.

Chemical balance of the body also gets disturbed,
Nervous system of the person is also perturbed.
It may cause diabetes and heart troubles,
May causes ulcer or mental troubles.

Forgive and forget is the most sweet revenge,
It ends enmity and vicious cycle of enmity ends.
What is the use of that revenge causing immense harm to your body,
Why not forgive and forget to make happy every body.

To forgive and forget is a rule divine,
To attain peace of mind, it is like a goldn mine.
Revenge often appears to be spuriously sweet,
Really it is a poison whose nature appears sweet.

A sensible person never believes in taking any revenge,
Forgiveness is far better than taking any revenge.

17. How to Relax your Body and Mind

Relaxation is very important for our body,
It acts like a panacea to cure a tired and weary body.
It is a gift of God to keep fit our mind and body,
Those who don't know this secret often slow poison their body.

To sleep at night and siesta at noon are its main parts,
Both refresh our body and mind to make a good start,
You must learn how to throw off responsibilities to enjoy sound sleep,
It is a skill which must be learned to have a sound sleep.

Stretch out comfortably your entire body,
Then concentrate on relaxing each part of the body.
Start from your head and reach upto toe,
Ask each muscle to loosen up and bow.

Consider your entire body as a dead log,
Lay still for a while like a frog.
To relax your mind recall any pleasant incident of the past,
You would start feeling relaxation in all body parts.

Now breathe slowly and steadily to relax your nerves,
Concentrate on incoming and outgoing breath forming curves.
It may be done to regain lost energy or to go to sleep,
It will rid you from that tension due to which you want to weep.

Relaxation is a skill which you must learn,
It is a must if you want good health to earn.
Meditation is a best way to relax a tired body.
Breathing exercises can also relax a tired and weary body.

18. Worry is a Live Grave

Worry is a live grave, why do you worry,
It can't solve any problem, then why do you worry.
Worry is the main cause of stress and strain,
Worry is the main cause of your heart pain,

Worry is the cause of many body troubles,
Worry is the cause of many mental troubles.
It increases mental tension very very high,
It increases blood pressure very very high,

It increases your anger very very high,
It increases frustration very very high.
Many of your fears are just imagination,
Many of your fears are just hallucination.

Why not kick them out to remove your tension,
What are the real reasons try to mention.
Family problems may be the cause of your worry,
Money problems may be the cause of your worry.

Frustration or fear may be the cause of your worry,
Resentment or anxiety may be the cause of your worry.
Stop thinking about worries and have peace of mind,
How much they can harm you, guess in your mind.

What can't be cured must be endured always keep in mind,
Engage yourself in any work, don't keep empty mind.
Count God's blessings to you and feel happy,
Rationalize your worries and feel happy,
Leave yourself to the will of God and feel happy,
Accept the things you can't change and feel happy.

Life is a beautiful gift of God with fortunes and adversities,
Life is not to waste for useless trivialities.

Life is not an imagination, but full of realities,
Life is what you can make it hell or modesty.
Life is very short why waste in worries,
If you love life then never never worry.

Shed away your worries and try to feel happy,
Let us sing and dance and feel very happy.
Worry is a live grave, why do you worry,
It is the root cause of sickness, why do you worry.

19. Passion

When one sees a beautiful woman, one wants to talk to her,
After talking one desires just to touch her,
After touching one desires to unite with her,
Then a strange passion arises in him for her.

20. What Causes Ulcer

Stomach ulcer is a fatal disease to kill any person,
It is found throughout the world and may attack any person.
The cause of stomach ulcer is not what we eat,
But what is eating us, and we can't beat.

Fear, worry, selfishness and hatred are the main causes,
Inability to adjust oneself to the real world, are also the causes.
Fear causes worry and worry causes tension,
And affects the nerves of the stomach as a reaction.

Then normal gastric juices are changed into abnormal,
And lead to stomach ulcer, which is quite normal.
Its prey are those who can't control their emotional outburst,
Loves rich people the most, who have one or the other lust.

At the cost of ulcer no use to earn any wealth,
Useless to gain even the whole world, at the cost of health.
Dishonesty and ill-will are the patrons of the ulcer,
Only right living and right thinking can save us from the ulcer.

21. Insomnia is a Psychological Disease

A few tired people go to sleep even while walking,
"I am unable to sleep", I often hear many people talking.
No one ever died due to lack of sleep,
None will die due to lack of sleep.

Many insomaniacs often sleep more than they realize,
But never come to know even for a while.
Worry about insomnia causes more damage than sleeplessness,
Physical work can save you from sleeplessness.

A relaxed body automatically invites a sound sleep,
Learn to relax all parts of your body to have a sound sleep.
Don't worry if you find it difficult to enjoy sound sleep,
Don't take medicines or drugs to have a regular sleep.

Medicines and drugs may produce side-effect,
Nature itself takes care of sleep, it is also a fact.
Those who lead a very comfortable life, find it difficult to enjoy sleep,
Those who exhaust their body by doing work, enjoy a sound sleep.

Learn the art of relaxation to enjoy a sound sleep,
That is a good panacea to have a sound sleep.
Insomnia is mainly a psychological malady,
Don't try to treat it as a biological malady.

Fear and suspicion are also the enemies of sleep,
Try to avoid them to enjoy a sound sleep.
When you find it difficult to go to sleep,
Lie down with closed eyes to invite sleep.

Start any type of meditation in your mind,
Concentrate on the name of your God in your mind.
You will surely go to sleep after some time,
Without knowing what you were doing in your mind.

If you do not believe in meditation,
Then learn the art of deep relaxation.
Feeling of security is a must to have a sound sleep.
Without security none can enjoy a sound sleep.

22. Law of Compensation

Law of compensation proceeds our life,
More we give more comeback greatly multiplied.
True wealth is not that which we grab from others,
It is something we build ourself out of service to others.

Riches not shared with others wither and die,
Nature makes all the things not in use to decay and die.
You acquire money through the efforts of others,
Then why not share with them to make happy others.

Teach others what you want to learn in life,
It will help you to learn more and become wise in life.

23. Happiness is Very Rare

Happiness is very rare in human life,
Why not feel happy and lead a happy life.
Shed away sadness and feel happy,
Happy, happy, happy, happy try to be happy.

Happiness can remove your tension of mind,
It can remove fatigues of many kinds.
Happiness provides us a very rare bliss,
And gives pleasure like a lover's kiss.

Compells the brain to release catecholamine,
Which in turn releases endorphin.
A natural pain killer of strange kind,
Which boosts the heart, body and our mind.

It purifies our heart and mind,
Takes away troubles of body and mind.
When it costs nothing, why not feel happy,
To enjoy a happy life why not feel happy.

Sing or dance and feel happy,
Happy, happy, happy, happy, always feel happy.
If you think ill of others, you will never be happy,
Always think good of others and feel happy.

The easiest way to be happy is to make others happy,
That happiness will return back to make you happy.
Happiness is contagious never comes directly,
When you give to others, it comes back indirectly.

24. Laughter is a Jogging for Mind and Heart

Laughter is a jogging for mind and heart,
Why not you then laugh from the core of your heart?
Those who can laugh for fifteen minutes a day,
Can enjoy a sound sleep and keep the doctor away.

It activates the heart and heart beat increases,
Amplifies respiration and heart attack decreases.
It triggers the brain to release catecholamine,
Which is a hormone of unique kind.

A natural pain killer of very strange kind,
It boosts the heart, body and the mind.
Highest form of laughter is to laugh at own follies,
Lowest form is to laugh at others' follies.

Never mind if anybody makes a fun of you,
That occassion can also entertain you.
Humour is a natural way to heal body and mind,
A best way to decrease stress from the mind.

If you want to live healthy, then laugh, laugh and laugh,
If you want a longer life then laugh, laugh and laugh.
Laughter is a rare gift of God to you,
To keep mind and heart fit for you.

Don't be a miser, when you laugh,
Don't miss any chance when you can laugh.
It costs nothing on your part,
Then why don't you laugh from the core of your heart.

It can make your heart to feel strong and healthy,
It is your rare possession even if you are not wealthy.

25. How to Avoid Heart Attack

Heart in human body is the most delicate part,
The lovers feel their love through this part.
But heart-attack is the most dreadful disease,
People are dying like flies due to this disease.

It is also the most powerful muscle,
To protect us in hustle and bustle.
It produces all the energy that our body needs,
The person may be a weight lifter or a lazy in little need.

If all the energy produced by heart is accumulated,
It can move even an engine if properly regulated.
But the power of evil thoughts is more powerful than the heart's power,
Heart produces constructive but evil thoughts produce destructive power.

Anger, fear, worry, ill-will and stress when long held in mind,
The vast power of the heart is greatly undermined.
These produce chemical imbalance in our body,
Pituitary and adrenal glands pour out hormones to save the body.

For a short time they succeed to bring the imbalance down,
But ultimately defence system itself breaks down.
Heart loses resiliency, arteries harden and BP rises,
Symptoms of heart attack develop and arthritis strikes.

The only anti-coagulant to avoid them is the peace of mind,
Money can buy many things but not peace of mind.
Drugs also can not provide real peace of mind,
Wine and whisky can't provide solace of any kind.

Emotional management can help, to attain peace of mind,
Contentment is also a remedy to gain peace of mind.
Happiness is the panacea to keep the heart healthy,
But real happiness comes only to the pure heart, a poor or a wealthy.

26. From *Ishawasya Upanishad*

It is wrong to desire to live without doing work in life,
Covetousness is caused due to desire to live an easy life.
Live your life by carrying on incessant work,
Life becomes a burden when one always shirks off work.

People suffer when they act in that way,
Much of the sins in the world are due to the desire to live in easy way.

27. Death is Inevitable

You like me or hate me, but can't avoid me,
None can tell exact time of me.
Ignorant people show their hatred towards me,
And always feel afraid of me.

I am like an unwelcome guest,
Even then a new life I always beget.
Old age is my sister and illness is my brother,
But none can escape from my net, may be a sister or a brother.

28. God may Forgive, But Nervous System Never

God may forgive many of your sins, but nervous system never,
Nervous system is always harmed when thinking ill-will ever.
A nursed grudge is like a cobra always keep in mind,
It can kill very easily your peace of mind.

Never confuse today's profits with life time peace of mind,
Spoken words come back to bless or curse our mind.
Ill-will is the cause of mental stress and strain,
Anger, hate and greed also cause pain.

Resentment and covetousness may cause heart attack,
Joy is a panacea to stop such attacks.
Right thinking and right living is the way to get joy,
Right eating and right behaving help to get joy.

All is well that ends well is the rule divine,
Keep these few things always in your mind.
One fit of anger may greatly damage your nervous system,
Then it takes many days to restore that nervous system.

What is the use of such anger and hate, which can spoil your
        health,
And may prove costly for your health and wealth.
Ill-will is a sick-will which is your foe,
Try to avoid them, all the greatmen advise so.

29. Fear of Old Age & Death

People often fear from old age and death,
When both are inevitable why not treat them with respect.
> *Old age may be a handicap in certain activities,*
> *Nature rewards it with other activities.*

Never takes away anything without compensation,
Provides experience and wisdom as compensation.
> *Old people feel helpless, due to thinking of their mind,*
> *Due to inferiority of any kind.*

Old age is the time to lead a religious life,
To thank the God for giving you this life.
> *Fear of death also disturbs the mind,*
> *When it is a inevitable, why do you mind.*

None ever lived forever in the whole world,
None would live for ever in the whole world.
> *Those who have born, must have to die,*
> *It is a reality and not a surprise.*

Death is the will of God none can avoid,
Why fearing death which happiness devoid.
> *What can't be cured must be endured is the rule divine,*
> *Then why fearing death and disturbing your mind.*

You can become immortal by doing good deeds,
By selfless service and serving those in need.
> *Nothing you brought here, nothing will take away.*
> *Except a false satisfaction from whatever you say.*

Family friends and kinsmen can't accompany anybody,
Everyone departs alone even leaving own physical body.

30. What Causes Unhappiness

EVERY body has problems in daily life,
May be about health, wealth, children, husband or wife.
Lack of health makes many feel bad,
Lack of wealth makes many feel sad.

Ungrateful children make many feel unhappy,
A few have no child so, they always feel unhappy.
Lack of money makes many feel miserable,
A few are very rich, even then feel miserable.

Unfaithful husband or wife makes each other sad,
Due to nagging, wife and husband both feel bad.
Cruelty of the husband makes the wife unhappy,
A bully wife makes the husband always feel unhappy.

Dis-harmony in family life makes the people unhappy,
forcing a divorce makes many feel unhappy.
Easiest way to be happy is to make others happy,
When you sow happiness you start feeling happy.

To gain something, you have to lose something,
Keep it in mind if you want to gain something.
Desires can't be quenched by only enjoyment,
Go on increasing with every enjoyment.

Discipline of mind and tongue can make you happy,
Contentment is the surest way to feel happy.
Health, wealth, beauty and youth never last longer,
Poverty and sickness also never last longer.

Due to over attachment many feel unhappy,
Attachment is also a cause to make us unhappy.
These are the part and parcel of human life,
To provide pleasure and pain in real life.

31. Riches & Peace of Mind

If you have mastered money, you may have peace of mind,
If money have mastered you, you won't have peace of mind.
A rose on a severed stem must have to die,
It can't remain there for a long time to lie.

Inaction and disuse lead to death and decay,
This nature's law applies without any delay,
Riches not shared with others meet the same fate,
It may happen soon or a little late.

You acquired your riches with the efforts of others,
Why not share with them as sisters and brothers.
Then your money won't devoid you from getting peace of mind,
But surely help you to attain peace of mind.

True wealth is not that which you grab from others,
It is something which you build by serving others.

32. Why Money is the God

Man thinks money is the best friend in life,
But money refuses to accompany even upto graveyard after life.
Relatives and friends also refuse to accompany beyond graveyard,
But good deeds always accompany even beyond graveyard.

Why money is the god of earth and sky,
Money is the dust that blinds all eyes.
Money makes the mare go, everybody knows,
Money is the power that makes the people bow.

Money brings respect in circle and society,
Money brings respect in relations and party,
Money brings respect in business and hotel,
Money brings respect in office and motel.

Money converts a foreign land into a native land,
Poverty turns the native land into a strange land.
Money helps to enjoy all pleasures of life,
Money helps to enjoy all comforts of life.

In a limit money is a must for life,
After limit it becomes a curse for life.
It attracts many selfish fair weather friends,
Who always misguide to meet their selfish ends.

It attracts swindlers, crooks, dacoits and robbers,
It attracts criminals and kidnappers but never people sober.
It attracts bad elements in the society,
Who have no respect for the people of piety.

Then money creates many tensions in human life,
What was once giving comforts, then become strife.
People lose contentment and peace of mind,
Body catches ailments of many kinds.

Money can buy a very big mansion, a small home can't it buy,
It can buy the most beautiful woman, a contented wife can't it buy.
It can buy most handsome youngman,
        a faithful husband can't buy,
It can buy many selfish people, a good friend can't it buy.

You were born empty hands and empty hands would die,
Nothing will go with you, every thing remain here lie.
Why to gather illgotten wealth which is nine days wonder,
Everything will have to here must surrender.

Contented wife and peaceful life is more than a million,
If you don't have these things, no use to earn even billion.
Purpose of the money is just to lead a happy life,
Your life is useless if have no harmony with wife.

33. From *Ishawasya Upanishad*

All kind of knowledge is not at all needed,
Only some kind of knowledge in life is needed.
One must learn what kind of knowledge is required,
And what kind of knowledge is not required.

Life remains disturbed by useless knowledge,
Will also remain disturbed due to lack of knowledge.

34. Conscience Guides and Misguides

Conscience is the moral guide of human mind,
It harmonizes the moral laws of nature and of mankind.
Its purpose is to modify individual's aim in life,
To help to take right decision in any predicament in life.

It is the twin brother of faculty of reason,
Whenever any reason is in doubt, it guides that reason.
It is also very naughty and has a strange quality,
It has the dual nature which is also a reality.

It gives guidance so long as its mandate is respected,
It refuses to guide if its mandate is rejected.
Then it becomes a conspirator in such cases as per its habit,
And starts justifying even the most destructive habit.

That is how bad people justify all their bad actions,
After doing heinous crimes, they neither repent nor show any reaction.
Those who obey its mandate may enjoy peace of mind,
Those who disobey, find themselves in disturbed state of mind.

35. From *Ishwasya Upanishad*

Those who forget God and hunt for pleasure seeking life,
Spurn the dignity of labour and lead an easy life,
Destroy their potential finer self,
And pave the way for the hell themselves.

Man has built many barriers between man and man,
It is causing strife in society, state, family and in man,
This can be eliminated with the true knowledge of God,
But only a true devotee can get this fruit from the God.

36. From *Ishawasya Upanishad*

Knowledge is necessary as well as ignorance,
What is not necessary, let that remain in ignorance.
If useless knowledge had been acquired that should be forgotten,
Don't pay any heed, let it should be rotten.

By following it, the wisdom becomes centred in God,
By not following it, one goes away from the God.
Knowledge and ignorance are part and parcel of life,
But some kind of knowledge is a must to become successful in life.

37. Stress is an Imp

It is difficult to find any person without stress and strain,
And claiming that in his body there is no sickness or pain.
Modern life is very strange,
It is full of stresses and strains.

These are like the imp of the bottle,
Which plays havoc when comes out of the bottle.
Stress and strain cause chemical imbalance in the body,
Which is the root cause of sickness in our body.

Chemical balance is controlled by pituitary and two adrenal glands,
These are located near the brain and kidneys of the man.
As per their duty these try to adapt the body against stress and strain,
To save the body from the impending pains.

Pour out hormones to bring the stress down,
For a while succeed but ultimately defence system itself breaks down.
Causing arteries to harden and blood pressure to rise,
Heart diseases develop and arthritis strikes.

Also encourage ulcer, cancer, and many other diseases.
And try to fill the body with a number of diseases.
If you want to enjoy a happy and longer life,
Learn to live without hurry and worry in real life.

Try to avoid ill-will, fear, hate and anger,
Deceit, avarice, covetousness and lust no longer.
Right living and right thinking is the best way of life,
Try to lead your life without any fuss or strife.

It can keep the imp of the stress shut off in the bottle,
Otherwise it is sure to come out of the bottle.

38. Sensuous Pleasure is Not Pure Love

A husband loves his wife not for his wife,
But to enjoy sensuous pleasures from his wife.
If leprosy or small pox destroys her beauty,
Then he will try to avoid her in all his duties.

To love some one to attain something is the selfish love,
Love for the sake of love is the true love.
Love of the body or skin is a passion of strange kind,
Love of God is a devotion which comes from the mind.

Pure love redeems and purifies the heart,
Transmutes into divinity to make a right start.
Love is the master key to open the door of eternal bliss,
It is that delight which none would like to miss.

But A drop of sensual pleasure is always mixed with a pail of pain,
Why people think it a very big gain.
Craving is the cause of sorrow and pain,
Why not keep it under control when nothing you gain.

Good or bad are only the thinking of the mind,
Something good may be bad in some other's mind.
When anybody rebukes, taunts or insults, don't lose heart,
It is only a play of words and sounds on his part.

A few terrible vices in human mind always breed,
Lust, anger, arrogance, affection, egoism and greed.
All religions advise how to keep them under control,
These prove the worst enemies if are not controlled.

When these are under control, one feels a calm mind,
And proves a spring-board to attain peace of mind.

39. Tension is a Modern Malady

Tension is a modern malady difficult to escape,
It follows everywhere sleeping or awake.
It is like a king cobra whose poison never fails,
People suffering from this malady can never hail.

Hurry & worry always produce very big tension,
Fear and anger always produce very big tension.
Marital quarrels also produce very big tension,
To meddle with the lives of others is also a cause of tension.

Ungrateful children may also be a cause of your tension,
Malice and envy is also a cause of mental tension.
Covetousness also produces a very big tension,
Family problems may also be a cause of your tension.

Job problems may be a cause of your tension,
Money problems may also be a cause of your tension.
False pride is also a cause of your tension,
People drink wine & whisky to avoid tension.

Some take dope and drugs to avoid tension,
Many take intoxicants to avoid tension.
Ultimately they increase their tension, while avoiding tension.

Tension causes chemical imbalance in our body,
Our glands secrete hormones to keep in check that tension.
Those hormones help to decrease the tension.
For a while they succeed to bring the imbalance down,
But ultimately defence system itself breaks down.

Heart muscle loses resiliency, arteries harden and BP rise,
Heart attack develops and arthritis strike,
Then encourage ulcer, cancer and many diseases,
And try to fill the body with many strange diseases.

Right living and right thinking is the best way of life,
Try to live a peaceful and happy life.
If you want to enjoy a happy and longer life,
Try to avoid tension in your life.

40. Let Go All Your Worries to Attain Peace

If you want real peace, always keep in mind,
You will have to cultivate peace in your heart and mind.
Remove the weeds of lust, hatred and greed,
Anger, selfishness and jealousy should also not breed.

Wealth, sex and wine can't give real peace,
These are the enemies of the peace.
Peep in the inner chamber of your heart,
Remove suspicion and prejudice from that part.

Greed for power and possession always disturbs the mind,
Let go all the worries from your mind.
Enlightenment and God never come from out side,
Are already within you awaiting to be discovered by.

Though these are inner core of our being,
Yet are separate from body, mind and individual beings.
This is the secret of the most secret teaching,
God is within you is the main teaching.

41. Ill-gotten Wealth Can't Provide Real Happiness

Ill-gotten wealth can't provide real happiness in life,
But becomes the cause of unhappiness in life.
It never comes alone to any person,
Her hordes of servants also accompany her to that person.

By nature those servants are the crooks,
They try to spoil the person by hook or by crook.
Lust, anger, greed, worry and jealousy are their names,
Egoism, vanity, attachment and pride are their fames.

These are the worms of the body and heart,
Carry on making weak all delicate body parts.
Even a single moment of one's life,
Wealth of the whole world can not buy.

Money can buy the most costly bed that you like,
But can't buy the sound sleep that you also like.
It can easily spoil your own children.
Ill-gotten wealth is only the nine days wonder,
It is like that whore that can make you asunder.

42. How to Be Successful in Life

If you want to be successful in your life,
Then you must heed to my advice.
Never rebuke or nag; it ends in futility,
Only speak good of others, it has utility.

Feeling of importance is very strong desire,
For this purpose people can face difficulties and ire.
Appreciate honestly and achieve many wonders,
Talk about what others want, keep yourself under.

Never say you are wrong and I am right ever,
Respect other's opinion, use your argument never.
Try to see the things from others point of view,
If you have different opinion, then you must review.

Everybody expects some sympathy from others,
Either he is a third person or your brother.
Begin with praise before pointing to mistakes,
Before criticising others, talk about your own mistakes.

People often hate to take all kinds of orders,
Why not ask questions, instead of giving direct orders.
If you want to keep your homelife happy,
Never nag your partner and be happy.

Don't criticize your partner before other people,
Appreciate good things before other people.
If you want friends let your friends excel,
If you want enemies, only then you excel.

Don't ride rough shod over the feelings of others,
May be a stranger or may be your own brothers.
Try to understand others to avoid friction,
Misunderstanding is also a cause of friction.

It will sow the seed of harmony and co-operation,
Will help to make new friends and new relations.

43. Problems

Everybody has problems one or the other,
To solve them takes the help of the others,
Some lack children, beauty or health,
Some want more power, prestige and wealth.

Some fear an enemy or displeasure of the ruler most,
Some want to avoid that nuisance which trouble them most.
Most people remain always unhappy,
Sincerely they never try to become happy.

44. Rama Krishna Says

The world is full of temptation, mind can break discipline,
But perfect man is that whose mind is under discipline.
A mud fish lives in muddy water but is not soiled,
This world is like muddy water, learn to live without getting soiled.

45. From the *Bhagavad Gita**

What you are holding will not be yours by tomorrow,
You got it from others, will go to others by morrow.
What happened or happening is for the better,
In future also will happen for the better.

Change is the continuing process of the world,
Changes are taking place every moment in the world.
What you see now, may not be by tomorrow in the world,
Going going gone, is the rule of the world.

46. Happiness and Service are Interconnected

When you serve others, you feel better in mind,
Provided you have no selfish motive to grind.
It gives enjoyment of a very strange kind,
Which is a main step to attain peace of mind.

You can find many rich men who are not very happy,
You rarely find any person serving others but not feeling happy.
Even serving the ungrateful people provides us enjoyment,
Law of compensation sends back many fold enjoyment.

Always serve the others without selfish motive,
And get peace of mind without any notice.
Selfless service is the main secret to become happy,
Service with a selfish motive, can't make anybody happy.

---

* "The Song of the Lord"—a part of great epic Mahạbharatạ.

47. Who is My Best Friend?

Money can buy many luxuries and comforts for our life,
Even then it can't be regarded as a best friend in life.
It refuses to accompany the person even upto graveyard,
Friends and relatives also refuse to accompany beyond graveyard.

It is the good deeds only that follow a person for ever,
They are the most trusted and faithful friends and betray never,
Why not spare some time to do good deeds,
Which are really a friend in need is a friend indeed.

48. O Rich Man ! You Must Understand

Dear rich man ! you must understand,
How much money do you need in hand.
There should be some limit in your life,
To provide comforts and luxuries to family and wife.

To feel that you have really tasted the treats of life,
And to gain respectability in your social life.
Lack of money always destroys peace of mind,
But excess of money may also destroy peace of mind.

To protect the children from poverty is very wise,
But to shield them with a wall of money is never advised.
When children know, they will inherit a great amount of money,
They won't like to work hard to earn more money.

It will devoid them to learn life taught wisdom in life,
Which is a must to get true peace of mind in life.
We realize the value of health only when we fall ill,
Such facts are learnt only when we face life with a strong will.

49. Sex is Constructive and Destructive

God created sex as a constructive power,
Bad people misuse it as a destructive power.
It had already rolled many people in the dust,
It would still roll many more in the dust.

Like Science its use or misuse is in your hands,
How to use this sacred power is in your hands.
Enjoyment of sex is your own birth right,
You have to decide what is wrong and what is right.

Your conscience is the best guide in this direction,
Who am I to give you any instruction.
It attracts everybody young or old,
Its transmutation is also a strong power to hold.

It can produce many wonders in your life,
It may produce many miracles in your life.
It helps in focussing inward forces of mind,
Which is very rare thing in mankind.

50. Happy Home

Nagging and scolding may spoil home life,
Try to avoid it, to have a happy life.
These are like a king cobra, whose poison never fails,
It is easy to scold but difficult to hail.

It may spoil married life boyond any repair,
Making you repent forever, feeling very despair.
Appreciate honestly and have a happy home,
Courtesy is very helpful to have a happy home.

Recognition is a nice way to have a happy home,
Poison of suspicion may spoil your happy home.
When God will judge a person after the end of the days,
Why not say good things of others, why ill of them you say.

Sex urge also plays a very important part,
If you are lagging in it, why not make a start.

51. Mind

It is very difficult to control the mind,
It always behaves in a very strange kind.
It is the originator of our desires,
Man is a helpless toy in the hands of those desires.

Mind like wind can not be controlled,
But through proper practice it can be controlled.
Holy men practice yoga to control the mind,

Many books are written on how to control the mind.

52. Motives Guide Our Actions

All our actions are guided by the motives,
May be a positive motive or any negative motive.
Positive motives are love, sex, money and self preservation,
Freedom, self expression and perpetuation.

Anger, revenge and fear are the negative motives,
Our life is dominated by these motives.
The roots of what we do or refrain to do is hidden in these motives,
Courts also decide the cases keeping in view the motives.

Positive motives may lead a person to have a happy life,
But negative motives are the hurdles in the way of a happy life.
Wise men try to avoid all the negative motives,
But mean people lead their lives with negative motives.

Misuse of negative motives also attract troubles,
And dissipate our mind into more troubles.
Love, sex and money are the main motives of the man,
They rule the whole world in whatever way they can.

53. Rama Krishna Says

Accumulated riches meet the fate of a bee hive,
Bees themselves never eat their own honey, but others loot the hive.
There are many who can give very good advice,
But there are only a few who care to follow a good advice.

54. Worry and Tension Cause Fatigue

Tiredness and weariness are sad aspects of life,
Many people complain about it in their whole life.
Many think that overwork is causing them fatigue,
But worry, tension and emotional upset are the causes of fatigue.

Your fatigue is probably centred somewhere in your mind,
It vanishes automatically when we refresh our mind.
When you think and affirm tiredness, you feel tired,
When you think and affirm energy you never feel tired.

Alive thinking always produces aliveness in the mind,
Never allow your thoughts to feel tiredness in your mind.
As you empty your pockets, learn to empty your mind,
It is a good method of relaxation of body and mind.

Relaxation is the absence of efforts and tension,
Tiredness disappears with the removal of the tension.

55. From *Bhagavad Gita*

Why crying? What have you lost in the world?
What is now yours, was with any other in the world.
You brought nothing, will take away nothing from here,
What you have lost was taken from here.

56. Intolerance is the Hidden Enemy

Intolerance is the hidden enemy of our mind,
It is the evil partner of selfishness and ignorance of mind.
It shuts out the facts and closes the mind,
Intolerant people always remain upset in their mind.

They can't win friends and influence people,
And can't get full co-operation of the people.
An intolerant person can't get peace of mind,
It always remains in the state of disturbed mind.

Intolerance is a weakness, while tolerance is a trait,
Tolerant people get admiration, while intolerant get hate.
Try to be tolerant if you want peace of mind,
Intolerant people can never get any peace of mind.

57. God

God is hidden inside your heart,
To find Him open the door of your heart.
As musk is hidden inside the deer,
But wanders here and there as is not clear.

God is also hidden inside the heart.
Remove your ignorance and see Him in your heart.

58. As You Sow, So You Reap

As you sow, so you reap,
This is the main theme all the religions preach.
Even then many people call it just a foolish talk,
As they find bad people flourishing in every walk.

They find bad people receiving respect in the society,
Which is not available to the good people of piety.
Honest people are sometime greatly shaken,
As they don't know how the society will be awaken.

Many bad people never realize the basic truth of life,
That Nature enforces its own laws to check the life.
In some cases it may take some time,
But none can prevent the Nature to take action in time.

When any body does any evil thinking or evil deed,
In its body a strange chemical imbalance is increased.
Pituitary and adrenal glands pour out hormones to save the
         body,
To maintain the balance and keep fit the body.

For a short time they succeed to bring the imbalance down,
But ultimately defence system itself breaks down.
Heart muscle loses resiliency, arteries harden and BP rise,
Symptoms of heart attack develop and arthritis strike.

And sows the seeds of many strange diseases,
Which gradually grow up as time increases.
Some are fatal, some slow poison the body,
This is the way of the Nature to give punishment to the body.

Evil thoughts and evil deeds always get punishment, keep it in mind,
Sooner or later account books are adjusted in a strange kind.
Never allow in your life evil thoughts to heap,
Because as you sow, so you will have to reap.

None ever escaped, none will escape in life,
Law of compensation takes its own course in life.

59. Worry and Tension Cause Malaise

Worry and tension are the main causes of malaise,
Try to control them to avoid that malaise.
There are some simple ways to avoid them,
Any body can learn easily how to avoid them.

Let us live each day as it comes our way,
Don't worry for the coming days that are on their way.
People always learn how to get rich, but never learn how to live life,
Which is causing sufferings to you and your wife.

Begin your day by liking everyone you meet,
Never become angry even if you don't have anything to eat.
Marital quarrels can cause ulcer, headache and pains,
Try to avoid them because you have nothing to gain.

Never go to bed angry with your wife or any other,
Try to adjust than finding faults with others.
Right living and right thinking is the best way in life,
This is the way to get peace of mind for you and your wife.

Quiet and serene life is very rare in these days,
Lust for more and more has changed our outlook these days.

60. How to Take a Decision

Living is like a science based on definite laws of nature,
Those who do not obey those laws, are punished by the nature.
Those who learn those laws, lead a happy and peaceful life,
But those who fail are always afflicted with many strifes.

Many people fail in life due to making wrong decisions,
As our life depends upon the outcome of those decisions.
Many people are often confused how to take a right decision,
A few go on postponing rather than taking any decision.

If your thoughts are based on prejudice, bias and fear,
You can not take a decision just and clear.
Personal opinion and emotional excitement often affect our decision,
Decision taken without examination of facts is often a wrong decision.

Many people are the victims of uncontrolled emotions,
They are not the masters but the servants of their emotions.
Self discipline helps a person to take a right decision,
An undisciplined person often takes a wrong decision.

Whenever you find it difficult to take any decision,
Your conscience can help you to take that decision.
Spiritual process may also help you in difficult matters,
Provided you are serious to take help in that matter.

Be seated at a quiet and lonely place for a short time,
After relaxing your body, and your mind.
*Now pray to **God** to send its guidance in that matter,*
Go on meditating unless you find a solution of that matter.

In the beginning you have to do it a number of times,
After mastery you will be able to do it in a short time.
Whether you are a theist or an atheist is not the main question,
Meditation with pure heart is the main question.

61. Don't be Afraid to Fail

Nothing ventured nothing gained,
Why not try again and again.
Don't feel afraid to take a chance due to any fear,
It is foolishness to be afraid to fail due to any fear.

No one can win a battle fought in a fear,
The biggest enemy of mankind is its imaginary fear.
Fear is the mother of our anxiety,
Doubt and indecision are the brothers of anxiety.

Anxiety often destroys our mental and physical health,
Paralyzes our knowledge which is our hidden wealth.
It strangles our initiative and destroys our skill,
Stifles our ingenuity and affects our will.

We suffer from that injustice which have not yet come,
It may be that, that injustice will never come.
Many of our fears are only imaginary and not in reality,
Imagination causes far more harm than a reality.

62. Meditation Can Help You in Many Ways

Meditation can help us in many ways in life,
To reflect, to ponder and to discover flaws in life.
The best way to relax body and mind is the meditation,
Heart also feels relaxed after meditation.

It helps to find out what is wrong in our mind,
And is easily available to the people of all kinds.
It is very helpful to those who sincerely want to improve,
Have the pluck and perseverence, and want to move.

It can easily set our inner house right,
And can pave the way to make us think right.
It helps us to discover our own soul,
And to set in motion the life's real goal.

It relieves us from stress and strain,
And helps to overcome many body pains.
It is the main tool of all the holy men,
To get salvation in the long run.

Meditation helps to awake inner spiritual powers,
To get peace of mind and to subdue develish powers.
TIME spent on meditation is not the time lost,
But increases the value of life at a very low cost.

During meditation one enters unique state of mind,
Which is very beneficial for body and mind.
When the rays of the mind are concentrated on a fixed point,
They produce wonders at that point.

It helps the nervous system to function in a normal way,
Provides a new energy to lead life in a happy way.
It also helps to keep away from alcohol and drugs,
When the mind feels calm, no use of such drugs.

63. Courtesy Oils Our Relations

Courtesy plays an important role in our life,
It works as oil to run our relations smoothly in life.
It is the mirror of our personality,
People guess from it our other qualities.

The best place to practise courtesy is our home,
Try it and feel how happy is your home.
Try courtesy on your husband or your wife,
Try it on your children and find surprises in life.

It is that quality of heart which greatly influences people,
They start liking you, may be they are good or bad people.
It clearly shows how civilized we are,
It also shows how respectful we are.

64. Hypochondria Prevents the Mind to Attain Good Health

Abnormal anxiety about one's health is very common,
Lazy people are its easy prey may be a man or a woman.
It is the offspring of luxurious and comfortable life,
Rich people are easily afflicted by it in their life.

Psychologists call it hypochondria you may name it any,
It is a psychological malady causing sufferings to many.
Some people are habitual grievance collectors in their mind,
They start their day by searching for symptoms of any kind.

They find many sure signs of illness with which to bore others,
They buy every quack remedy that comes along one or another.
They imagine illness, think illness, fear illness and bring illness,
Then their mind transmutes imaginary illness into real illness.

A lot of illness is caused due to unpeace of mind,
Most of them vanish automatically when you have peace of mind.
Headache, ulcers, indigestion, sleeplessness and kidney troubles,
Impotence, frigidity, fatigue and circulatory troubles.

These arise from mental conflicts, fears and tensions,
There are many more which may not be mentioned.
Think joy and have joy always keep in mind,
This is a secret to have health and peace of mind.

Hypochondria prevents the mind to attain good health,
If you have no health, then what is the use of your wealth.
If you are always thinking about the symptoms of any illness,
Your mind will transmute that thinking into real illness.

Think joy, affirm joy and feel joy,
This is the main secret if you want your life to enjoy.

65. Complexes Play Very Important Role

A complex is an unpleasant feeling of the past,
Which causes abnormal state of mind due to that past.
Complexes play very important role in human life,
By directing their actions throughout their life.

Anxiety, fear and nervousness are a few symptoms,
Timidity and phobias are also its symptoms.
A complex can easily ruin happiness in life,
By pushing a person into a definite path in life.

As these are connected with the sad feelings of the past,
No one likes to admit it and bring to light that past.
People always suppress them and protect themselves from them,
Make a compromise with life, not to suffer from them.

Although every body wants to avoid its bad effects,
Yet nervousness clearly shows its bad effects.
Whenever there is a conflict between conscious and subconscious
            mind,
It shows its effects through nervousness in mind.

Complexes can make us to suffer in life,
Can make it difficult to adjust in life.
A complex also gives birth to any anxiety,
In our subconscious it increases the anxiety.

Complexes develop a hidden personality of a separate kind,
In many actions they greatly influence our mind.
One must be strong and stable to cope with changing circumstances,

And need different approaches to tackle those circumstances.
Some people do such things which normally they won't like to
        do,
Because complexes compel them those things to do.
A complex is the secret of a subconscious mind,
A person suffering from complexes won't get peace of mind.

If you want to get rid of from your complexes,
Try to know the real cause of your complexes.

66. From *Bhagavad Gita*

Thou has a right only on your actions,
Thou has no right on the fruit of those actions.
Do all actions without attachment or motive,
The fruit of action should not be thy motive.

Do your work in a spirit of great sacrifice,
Perform your duty without attachment or price.
Craving and anger impel to do the sins,
Those who have gained wisdom can avoid those sins.

67. Revenge Increases Enmity

Revengefulness is a common trait found in mankind,
It is found throughout the world in the same kind.
A mighty person may take its revenge at the very moment,
A weak person may await for an appropriate moment.

Revenge increases enmity without end in sight,
As a chain reaction both the sides fight.
It provides only a momentary satisfaction,
But the vital parts of the body show strange reaction.

I want to draw your attention towards another aspect,
Which requires your full attention and you can't reject.
Revengefulness strangely disturbs our mind,
And causes psychosomatic disease of any kind.

Chemical balance of the body also gets disturbed,
Nervous system of the person is also perturbed.
It may cause diabetes and heart troubles,
May cause ulcer or mental troubles.

Forgive and forget is the most sweet revenge,
It ends enmity and vicious cycle of enmity ends.
What is the use of that revenge causing immense harm to your body,
Why not forgive and forget to make happy every body.

68. Save Yourself From Anxiety

Anxiety and worry are the twin brothers,
Fear is their father and mind is their mother.
When we feel troubled due to fear of uncertainty,
That state of mind is called anxiety.

As weapons are a menace to the world peace,
Anxiety is a menace to the mind's peace.
The sufferer feels afraid of many things real or unreal,
Anticipates troubles which may not be real.

Throat dries up, heart beat increases,
Starts trembling and spasm increases.
Those who live on their nerves, easily become anxiety ridden,
Peace of mind for them is always forbidden.

Although that fear is not real but fear syndrome is there,
The person fears from that danger which is really not there.
Base of the fear is generally known as real,
But anxiety is always based on something not real.

In the fear the enemy is known and one can fight,
But in anxiety the enemy is hidden and not in sight.
It is an intensive form of tension causing many side effects,
Choked throat, dumbness and urine discharge are the main effects.

Indigestion, stammering, palpitation are also its side effects,
Convulsion, vomiting, trembling and hysteria are also its effects.
It is very difficult to find any man free from anxiety,
Because none can progress in life without normal anxiety.

It is not a sign of cowardice in life,
It borns from uncertainty in human life.
Modern life predisposes us to fatigue, over-work and agitation,
Causing depression and mental agitation.

We have to fight noise, competition and other disturbances,
Which may cause physical and mental disturbances.
A timid person may easily become a victim of anxiety,
And adopts many facades to protect himself from that anxiety.

Some people buy things beyond financial means in life,
Then face fears, anxiety and tension in life.
Opposed and contradictory feelings also cause anxiety,
Physical troubles of the person may also cause anxiety.

Many people suffer from anxiety throughout their lives,
But they never come to know about it in their whole life.
It remains hidden in their subconscious mind,
That is why it also disturbs peace of mind.

People produce their own defence methods to fight anxiety,
Some drink liquor, some take tranquilizers to fight anxiety.
If anybody has anxiety from other people,
Will try to avoid to meet those people.

Some start feeling inferiority and timidness against other people,
Which prevent them to compete with other people.
They develop timidity to escape from circumstances causing anxiety,
Unconsciously they adopt these measures to fight anxiety.

Hypochondria, insomnia, guilt feeling are kinds of anxiety,
Complexes and neurosis are also a form of anxiety.
Feelings of inferiority make it difficult to face life,
Which ultimately deforms our personality in life.

Some develop false ways to show their superiority,
Just to show the people that they have no inferiority.
When they feel humiliation, try to humiliate others,
Use this facade to protect themselves in the eyes of others.

They try to maintain that facade at any price,
Even if they have to pay a very big price.
Try to find the real cause of anxiety in your mind,
Then try to eliminate it from your mind.

Keep your mind occupied to distract from anxiety,
Don't rest but work hard to avoid anxiety.
T.V., radio, music, gymnastis and journey help to distract the mind,
Empty mind always magnifies more anxiety in the mind.

Normal anxieties are part and parcel of our life,
But abnormal anxiety always disturbs our life.
An anxiety ridden person creates a strange atmosphere around him,
Which affects all the persons living around him.

69. Grievance Collector Can't Attain Peace

Don't become a grievance collector in your life,
It obstructs to lead a happy and peaceful life,
To nurse grievances against anybody is a bad habit,
Many destroy their peace of mind due to this habit.

It only creates prickly conditions in life,
Which then disturb our peace in life.
Then we say only those things which are ill advised,
It deprives us to develop our own inner power to rise.

Collection of grievances act like a slow poison,
It can harm your nervous system with that poison.
It often encourages ulcer like disease,
Or as a reaction, any other disease.

It is better to express one's grievances at any appropriate time,
Than to go on nursing it in your mind.
It will help you to throw out accumulated poison,
You will feel peace after vomiting that poison.

Try to forget any injustice done to you,
To get dignity and peace of mind, it will help you.
You will be able to absorb criticism and attack of any jealous person,
It will help you to gain the understanding and esteem of all good persons.

Collection of grievances is like poisoning the body,
Slow poisoning oneself would not be liked by anybody.
Avoid grievance collection to protect your life,
It only creates prickly conditions in your life.

70. Self Interest is the Main Interest

Self interest plays a very important role in life,
It makes friends and foes in life.
In no time it can change a friend into a foe,
None can be forever a friend or a foe.

The moment the interest clashes the friend seems as a foe,
No one in the world is a permanent friend or foe.
People get united out of selfish motives,
And become friends to achieve that motive.

No one pays any heed when interest is over,
Interest automatically ceases, when work is over.
Children also discard their parents when their interests are over,
Relations pay no attention, when their motive is over.

This is the world of self interest, don't feel hurt,
It is quite natural don't lose heart.
Selfishness is the part and parcel of the world,
One can find it everywhere in the whole world.

71. Sense of Guilt Deprives Peace

Sense of guilt deprives us peace of mind,
Try to eliminate it from your mind.
Have spiritual operation of your mind,
And remove all moral festers from your mind.

Ask a very simple question from your mind,
Am I doing anything wrong of any kind?
As soon as the moral wrong goes out; peace will enter,
You will feel a great change in your mind's centre.

Old sins create a deep sense of guilt in future life,
Causing fears and tensions for a long time in life.
Remove your sense of guilt if you want peace of mind,
Otherwise it will harm your body and mind.

72. O Dear Fellow !

O, dear fellow! would you please mind,
If I dare to make you remind.
Strife, violence, licentiousness and materialism,
Lustful living and hedonism.

Is not a right living and not the real goal of life,
These only make us, to waste the most precious life.
None can get real peace with this kind of life,
You will be only decaying your valuable life.

God has bestowed you with hidden spiritual powers,
Real peace can be attained after arousing those powers.

73. Scandals and Scounderals are Very Common

There remained always evil natured men,
Even Gods were persecuted by such men.
These are the part and parcel of this world,
They are the ignoble persons of this world.

They spare no one from their dirty work,
They always continue their ignoble works.
When even Gods had to suffer from their hands,
How can an ordinary person remain safe from their hands.

None can correct this tamsic portion of the world,
They will continue creating mischief in the whole world.
For humanity they are also a blessing in disguise,
People come to know about the noble aspect of life.

74. Ill Will is the Cause of Ill Healh

Ill will is the cause of your ill health,
Even then many people like it more than the real wealth.
When you allow ill will to accumulate in your mind,
Its inevitable accompaniment of guilt then clogs the mind.

Then the natural vital powers are greatly depressed,
Then in the mind sick feelings are stressed.
Goodwill is the antidote to remove ill will,
It has healing qualities for your ill will.

75. Desires Can't be Satiated

Desires remain unsatiated in human life,
Even after possessing the wealth of the whole world in life.
Everyone is a helpless toy in the hands of desires,
The root cause of many troubles are our desires.

When a person desires for power, name and fame,
It leads to greed, jealousy, meanness and vain.
Desire for food, sleep and sex are common in every person,
Desires for worldly objects can bind in chains every person.

Externalization of the mind towards any object is the cause of desires,
Movement of the mind towards objects is called a desire.
Mind believes that a particular object can provide happiness,
Then it fully tries to attain that happiness.

Peace comes in the heart of a desireless person,
When senses and mind are controlled by that person.
People run madly after sensual pleasure,
But root cause of many troubles is the sensual pleasure.

While there are desires, there can't be peace,
As desires decrease, so increases peace.
People are more interested in food, sex and indolence,
It causes only due to their own ignorance.

Sensual pleasure is the sweet darling of the common people,
These can make even insane to many people.
Happiness lies in the mind and not in the wealth,
Mind feels happy with the happiness of soul and not with the wealth.

Main teachings of Lord Buddha is to cease desires,
The root cause of our un-happiness are our desires.

76. A Criticizer is a Friend and not a Foe

Vulgar people take delight in criticizing others,
Never realize how they are hurting the others.
A criticizer when criticizes, feels some importance,
And feels satisfaction of his own importance.

No one kicks a dead dog always keep in mind,
You have accomplished something which is disturbing criticizer's mind.
You should be thankful to a criticizer,
He has taken a note of you and is not a miser.

Only those are criticized who have some qualities,
No one flogs a dead horse, it is also a reality.
You can improve yourself in the light of criticism,
You should be indebted to him for that criticism.

People often lose their temper when they are criticized,
Governments also impose censorship when they are criticized.
People like flattery and hate to listen their own faults,
It is a human weakness not to listen to their own faults.

Treat a criticizer as a friend and not as a foe,
Has dared to say something about you so.
Don't feel nervous when anybody criticizes,
By improving yourself you can become more wise.

An unjust criticism is like a disguised compliment,
Due to your talent you are receiving such compliments.
Many seek mean spirited gratification by criticizing others,
They feel satisfaction while tearing down others.

Arrogant people feel envy and jealousy from progress of others,
May be relatives and friends or their own brothers.
It is habit of the people to unjustly criticize,
Don't feel disturbed when they unjustly criticize.

Ignore unjust criticism and never mind,
This is the way to maintain your own peace of mind.
If you are sure, whatever you are going to do is right,
Then don't feel afraid of being criticized.

You will be damned if you dare to do,
You will also be damned even if you don't dare to do.

77. Life is an Obstacle Race

Everybody has to run obstacle race in life,
None can escape, it is the reality of life.
Those who win, lead a serene and quiet life,
Those who lose, lead a very miserable life.

Ill-will, fear, hate, anger, greed and lust are the main hurdles,
Intolerance, envy and deceit are the other hurdles.
Peace of mind is the gold medal of this unique race,
Only a few are able to win any medal in this race.

When you can't avoid this race in your life,
Why not try to win any medal in your life.
Speed is not so important as are the hurdles,
Those who are pure in heart never bother for these hurdles.

You must have to cross these hurdles if you want peace of mind,
There is no other way to attain peace of mind.

78. Attachment *(Moha)* is Your Biggest Weakness

Attachment forbids a monkey not to throw away her dead child,
Can keep with her even for three months that dead child.
Does not bother about the bad smell coming out from that
*   skeleton,*
Does not believe that she is only carrying a skeleton.

That infatuated love is called attachment,
Very common in many persons is that attachment.
People love their own body, family and mother,
Father, sister, property and their brothers.

This attachment keeps the people binding to the world,
Due to that attachment no one likes to leave the world.
They are ready to forsake even heaven, due to worldly attachment,
None want to die due to worldly attachment.

Normal attachment is a must to carry on family life,
But abnormal attachment creates many abnormalities in life.
It becomes a hindrance in attaining peace of mind,
Weakens the will of the person to attain peace of mind.

Attachment is the biggest weakness of mankind,
It is like a net of very strange kind.

79. Shed Away Hypocrisy

Most of the people always live a double life,
They wear many types of masks and facades in real life.
They never show their real inner face to the people,
In this way they go on befooling the people.

This hypocrisy helps them to conceal their dirty acts,
To mislead the people about their real nature and conduct.
With this type of life they mainly befool themselves,
For this deception they have to show oversmart themselves.

This kind of false life devoid them to attain peace of mind,
As deception greatly affects their own inner mind.
It proves a hindrance in adopting an alternate way of life,
As they feel afraid to admit their past misdeeds of life.

It causes stress and strain in their life,
Which ultimately leads them to acquire any disease in life.
They also become an easy prey of any psychosomatic disease,
And become a fertile ground to develop any heart or ulcer like disease.

None can improve without tearing off the masks of hypocrisy,
To become a better individual one has to relinquish hypocrisy.
Right living and right thinking is the best way in life,
To enjoy peace and real treat of life.

80. Muscle Tension

Mental tension and muscle tension are the twin brothers,
Stress is their father and strain is their mother.
Illegally they occupy our mind's house,
One should try to evict them from that house.

Remove all moral festers from your mind,
By eliminating scruples of all kinds.
As mental tension leaves, muscle tension also follows,
And mind starts feeling relaxed and hollow.

81. Why People Become Insane

Anxiousness and harassment cause mental strain,
Unable to cope with, make them insane.
Realities of the world are very very hard,
Those who can't face it feel very retard.

Break off all their contacts with the real world,
Retract themselves into an imaginary world.
They start to live into their own dream world,
That is their way to solve the worries of the real world.

Some call them mad, some call them insane,
Some call them senseless, some without brain.
This is a defence mechanism adopted by the brain,
When they can't face the reality, they become insane.

82. Love Your Job

Place of work is a temple, and work is worship,
No worship is greater than this worship,
Enthusiasm and eagerness make the job thrilling,
Learn to like your job, even if you are not willing.

Your Job is providing you many comforts of life,
By loving your job you can attain peace in life.
You are serving many people through your job,
Fine example of selfless service is your job.

If you believe that in every life there resides God,
Then through your job, you are serving the real God.
Honest and sincere work is the easiest way to serve God,
Your salary is the immediate reward you are getting from God.

You can find many wealthy people not feeling happy,
But can't find any person serving selflessly, but not feeling happy.
If you are not working honestly for which you are paid,
Then even your salary is the ill-gotten wealth being made.

If you don't work according to the best capabilities that you hold,
It is a treachery of the abilities that you behold.

83. Faith and Health

Faith is a panacea to cure an incurable disease,
Can cure a serious illness and mental disease.
Have faith in your health to remain healthy,
Those who go on searching symptoms of illness, can never remain healthy.

Mind can transmute all beliefs into their physical forms,
And can make you ill from any disease of that form.
Never imagine illness, to protect yourself from illness,
When you develop image of illness, you surely acquire illness.

When you think tiredness you begin to feel tired,
But happily you can play for hours, without feeling tired.
Think energy, affirm energy, you will feel alive,
You will start feeling in mind a new type of drive.

84. Divine Nectar

Sensual pleasure is the main bone of contention,
These attract every body with good or bad intention.
These provide real pleasure to the common people,
These can make mad to many types of people.

85. Lord Buddha's Prescription

None can seek happiness through hurting others,
Happiness comes only when you love others.
You yourself fear death and fear pain,
Then why do you kill or cause others any pain.

Don't use harsh words and provoke others,
They may also pay you back in the same coin may be your brother.
Then it will produce anger in your mind,
And sufferings will follow of strange kinds.

Do as you wish to be done by,
Its the golden rule of the wise.
A person should not live heedlessly,
But should exert to live righteously.

86. Material Gains and Freedom

To gain material wealth, many give up freedom of mind,
They like material gains more than their freedom of mind.
Those who earn money through dishonest means,
Devoid themselves of the genuine joy which comes with honest means.
Our conscience is a witness in all our deals,
Inflicts reward or punishment according to the deeds.

87. By Befooling You Befool Yourself

You can easily befool others by using deceitful words,
And may feel happy on the success of those words.
Can you imagine, how much you have befooled yourself,
Actually you have only slow poisoned yourself.

That poison will go on increasing gradually in your nerves,
And will start harming your delicate nerves.
It may harm your stomach and your heart,
As both got unnatural food from the very start.

You have sown the seed of a strange internal disease,
It will start growing to become a major disease.
At an appropriate time it will show its result,
By causing any inner disease as a result.

You have harmed your nervous system unknowingly for ever,
God may forgive many of your sins, but your nervous system will
*   never.*
Every action has a reaction, always keep in mind,
Never befool anybody, in any way, or in any kind.

By befooling you get only fraudulent happiness,
What is the use to drink poison in the name of happiness.
Try to speak the truth to avoid such maladies,
Cleverness can't save you from those maladies.

Give and get is a very simple law of the nature,
Whenever you give something, you get back something from the nature.
To tell a lie is easy, to speak the truth is not so,
That is why you befool others expecting they will like so.

88. A Change of Heart

Once there was one of the most rich men of the world,
But he was also one of the most unhappy men in the world.
He always entertained avarice and greed in his mind,
As a result he developed many diseases of strange kind.

Doctors declared that he would not survive for more than 160 days,
His days were numbered come what may.
Despite best medicine and best medical advice,
He was unable to get any hope of his life.

Someone suggested him to use his extra money for welfare causes,
He acted on that advice and started taking interest in the welfare causes.
He realized that he earned money with the help of others,
It would be proper to use that money for the welfare of others.

All at once avarice disappeared from his mind.
He felt a strange change in his body and mind.
His health improved in a miraculous way,
The man who was going to die in 160 days lived for 12,000 more days.

Mr. Rockfeller was the name of that man,
After realizing his self, he became a changed man.
Real happiness does not lie in possessing the money,
Real happiness lies in the proper use of that money.

History is full of many such persons,
After realizing this secret they became changed persons.

89. Who is Happy He or Me?

I know a person many times more rich than me,
But is full of avarice and not contented like me.
Who is happy, he or me?

He drinks whisky with chicken every day,
But I refrain from such things come what may.
He eats more tasty and rich foods than me,
But can not digest food like me,
Then who is happy, he or me?

With his power of money, he enjoys sex for recreation,
But I believe in using the sex for procreation.
Sex should be enjoyed only in married life,
Licentiousness is not the right way of life.

He believes in hedonism, but I believe in altruism,
Then who is happy, he or me?
He uses all types of fair and foul means to earn money,
And is the slave of the money.

I also want to earn just sufficient money,
But not as a slave of the money.
Money is only a medium to fulfil our needs,
It becomes a cause of misdeeds when earned beyond needs.

Then it encourages lust, anger, hate and greed,
Ill will and jealousy also breed.

Then who is happy, he or me?
He wants to enjoy everything which can perceive with senses,
Wastes a lot of money to gratify his senses.
Real enjoyment does not lie in the enjoyment of senses,
But is hidden inside the body which is beyond senses.

It may be enjoyed without spending any money,
Then why to run madly to acquire ill-gotten money.
Money can provide many physical comforts in life,
But contentment only can provide real peace in life.

Then who is happy contented or the rich,
Real happiness comes to the contented and not to the rich.
Due to avarice he is always in stress and strain,
Mental worries are giving him many types of pains.

He can not sleep without taking the sleeping pills,
But I can sleep at a fixed time at my own will.
He thinks it a waste of time to do activities like meditation,
But I start my day with prayer and meditation.

Due to leading the most comfortable life, he is suffering from diseases,
High BP, headache, heart troubles and diabetes like diseases.
My hard and simple life enables me to keep away many diseases,
It is like a gift of God to me to keep away diseases.

Money and desires have a strange relation,
It is found equally in all the nations,
It is the main cause of disturbance of mind,
It always devoids peace of mind.

90. Happiness and Unhappiness Lie in Our Thinking

Everybody wants to become superior in the society,
wishes to be the centre of attraction in the society.
They want to have physical and economic powers,
They wish to have social and political powers.

Others should be dependent wholly on them,
No leaf should move, without the permission from them.
They want to become independent in all the spheres of life,
They want to be called wise, handsome and graceful in life.

If any of these things is not fulfilled in life,
They try to fulfil that in fantasies in life.
Some imagine to become president as they think themselves wise,
They will surely win any international prize.

They will marry the most beautiful woman in the world,
This is the imagination of many in the whole world.
This imagination is also one of the causes of unhappiness,
More one desires, more one feels unhappiness.

To remain happy one should adopt balanced thinking in mind,
Even in adverse condition one should not lose one's mind.
But a rich man can not keep a balanced mind in adverse conditions
and can't bear insult, injury and persecution.

Ambitions are a must to progress in life,
But superfluous ambitions can spoil the life.

91. Spiritual Way of Life

It is not very difficult to lead a spiritual life,
One has to make some adjustments in one's daily life.
No need to follow any specific religion,
As inner attitude is important than following any religion.

One has to acquire insight into the realities of the world,
How conflicting forces like good and evil are affecting the world.
All these are intertwined in the social fabric of the society,
One must appreciate the diversities found in the society.

One has to learn to play one's role in the society,
By contributing constructive and selfless services for the society.
Start your day in a dynamic and spiritual way,
By doing meditation regularly every day.

Concentrate upon the meaning of God as the dynamic world spirit,
With truth, freedom, welfare, creative action, try to realize your spirit.
Make a mental survey of all the activities you propose to do that day,
Rehearse within yourself how best you can do that day.

Perform them in accordance with the spiritual ideal of life,
Don't allow your daily schedule to be over-crowded in life.
Select carefully the important matters just enough for the day,
Set aside other things for the next day.

Perform those actions in the attitude of serving the divine.
For one's own self, society and the will of the divine.
Whenever you find a little free time in the course of the day,
Rededicate yourself as an instrument of the divine at least once a day.

Repeat the name of your God in your own mind,
You will feel divine protection in your mind.
Before retiring at night do a reflection or meditation,
Offering thanks to God for your good luck and recreation.

Such a spirit of thanksgiving would prevent vanity and pride,
Would prove a source of encouragement and without anything to
        hide.
Remembrance of God transmutes egotism into self esteem,
Encourages to adopt only fair and proper means.

Then make a comprehensive and critical review of activities of the
        day,
For some you may feel proud, for some you may feel sorry
        that day.
Don't allow your feelings to sour your life,
Find out what mistakes were made, to prevent them in future life.

After extracting lessons of the day, banish all thoughts from
        the mind,
Adopt a relaxed attitude and establish perfect silence in mind.
When you will adopt this kind of prayful attitude,
You will get a sound sleep, with that attitude.

God has bestowed man an innate faculty of knowledge,
One can discover the truth with that knowledge.

92. Contentment is The Best Solution

There is one virtue that many people know,
Even then they behave as they don't know.
When that virtue develops in our mind,
It leads the person to attain peace of mind.

That virtue enables the sages to live a carefree life,
It helps them to attain God in their life.
Contentment is the name of that virtue,
Everybody knows the value of that virtue.

It is a positive virtue and not a negative suppression,
It is a sublimating force and not a regression.
It can transmute desires and greed into a wish for realisation,
Provides detached outlook towards life to help God realisation.

It helps to rise above avarice and selfish limitations in life,
Provides moral strength to rise above petty ends in life.
Protects from hatred towards those who are better placed,
Saves from blind pursuit of material gains in mad race.

It does not discourage from ambitions in life,
And does not make you less active or lethargic in life.
It encourages to utilize energy in a proper way,
And to spend it in a more rational way.

It helps to develop a calm and pointed mind,
And to gain real peace in your mind.
The gross energy is transmuted into a moral force,
One can achieve higher values with that force.

A restless mind is like a poison which comes out from greed,
Contentment is an antidote to that poison of greed.
Meditation helps to attain contentment in mind,
To realize God and to attain peace of mind.

93. Coming To This World is Not in Your Own Hand

You had nothing to do with coming into this world,
You had nothing to do with leaving out from this world.
But you have many things to do to maintain your life,
You can be the master or the slave of your life.

You may be the captain of your soul by taking possession of your mind,
You can find out the ways to have peace of mind.
Try to master yourself than mastering others,
It brings unhappiness when one tries to meddle with the lives of others.

Your own mind is your master, always keep in mind,
You are bound only by the patterns you had set up in your mind.

94. Divorce Wrecks Family Life

A divorce may cause many anomalies in human life,
It shakes up the very foundation of a happy family life.
Less stigma is attached to it in the West,
As they treat the marriage just like a contract.

But in India marriage remained a sacrament and sacred act,
Husband and wife both take some oaths before this sacred act.
Husband promises to remain chaste like Lord Rama,
Wife promises to remain loyal as Sita to Rama.

She promises to serve him till the end of her life,
And to remain sincere to the core of her life.
She will realize God by serving him as God,
Will submit to him as a devotee submits to God.

The husband promises to remain loyal to her through thick and thin,
He shall always respect her and never kick up a din.
Materialistic thinking has greatly changed the concept of marriage,
Sexual gratification has become the main aim of the marriage.

Now people want variety in sex and beauty,
To lead a well settled life is not their aim or duty.
It is giving rise to many new problems,
Shattered homes is becoming a very acute problem.

Children have to suffer many pangs in life,
Fault of their parents is proving a curse in their life.
Clash between the egos is the main cause of the divorce,
By making rational adjustments one can avoid the divorce.

95. How to Fight Depression

Depression is very common in human life,
Many people face depression throughout the life.
A depressed person loses enthusiasm and feels sad,
Brings reproach to itself to feel bad.

The sufferer tries to gain sympathy, support and care,
If fails then shows rage then and there.
It may lead the person to commit suicide,
To frighten other people they often cry.

Sad occasions in life are the causes of depression,
Melancholy is also caused due to depression.
Try to think how you can make someone happy,
Due to its contagious nature, you will also start feeling happy.

Happiness is contagious, by giving you receive,
Provided it is selfless and not to deceive.
Take interest in others and help them as best as can you,
Whatever you give, will come back to you.

People will start respecting you from the core of their hearts,
You will receive praises from sincere hearts.
Selfless service is a panacea to get rid of depression,
Adopt it if you want to keep away depression.

Selfless service is also the main message of Gita,
Service without reward is the main teaching of Gita.
Karma Yoga is also based on this philosophy,
To get real enjoyment it is the real philosophy.

Try to do one good deed daily in your life,
It will surely bring peace in your sad life.

96. Count Blessings, Not Troubles

People often count their troubles, never count their blessings,
Troubles are very few in comparison with the blessings.
For our troubles we often complain to God,
But for boons and bounties we never thank God.

Think of the man who has no eyes or legs,
Think of the man who always begs,
Compare yourself with such unfortunate people,
Is not God more generous with you than those people?

People seldom think of what they have,
They always complain of what they do not have.
These kinds of thinking always disturb the mind,
And make it difficult to attain peace of mind.

Fortunes and misfortunes are the part and parcel of life,
Try to adjust yourself accordingly in your life.
What can't be cured must be endured, always keep in mind,
Accept it as the will of God and don't disturb your mind.

Every cloud has a silver lining too,
Only patience can bring comforts to you.
First count your blessings, then count your troubles,
Then you can face boldly all your troubles.

97. Keep Yourself Busy to Drive Away Worry

None can think more than one thing at a time,
Use it as a panacea to cure your worried mind.
One kind of emotion always drives out the other,
When the mind is busy, worry can't bother.

Interesting work always soothes the nerves,
And saves the mind to become disturbed.
As air rushes to fill vacuum places,
To fill the mind with any emotion the nature races.
There are many negative emotion.

Hate, fear, worry and jealousy are such emotions.
These negative thoughts try to destroy peace of mind,
These are the enemies of heart and mind.

Try to keep your mind busy with constructive thoughts.
Then peace of mind can easily be brought.
Many people have a habit to worry.
Keep your mind busy to break that habit of worry.

An empty mind is called the shop of the devil,
Keep your mind busy to avoid that devil.
Worry is a live grave, avoid all worries,
Keep yourself busy to avoid your worries.

98. It is Silly to Quarrel Over Trifles

Trifles cause unhappiness in human life,
Can sour the relationship between husband and wife.
These are the causes of many marital quarrels,
These are the causes of many social quarrels.

An insulting remark or a disparaging word may hurt any person,
Domestic wrangling, sheer bravado may hurt any person.
Trifles may also lead to assault and murders,
These are the causes of many useless murders.

Although it looks silly to quarrel over trifles,
Yet many quarrels take place due to the trifles.
Never become upset by small things,
Small trifles always unhappiness brings.

Always try to avoid all types of trifles,
One trifle often leads to any other trifle.
Don't lose your mind over any trifle,
Just laugh away after listening any trifle.

Trifle can very easily arouse your anger,
Many diseases are caused due to anger.
Don't react over trifles if you want peace,
Trifles are the hidden enemies of our peace.

99. Don't Fight With The Inevitable

Don't worry what is hidden in the store of your future,
Who knows what will happen in the future?
Do your work as best as you can do,
Don't worry what is written in the fate for you.

This is the main teaching of the Gita,
It was said by Lord Krishna to Arjuna in the Gita.
The future is affected by many forces,
None can tell who prompts all those forces.

Don't worry about things which are beyond your power,
Leave those things to the Almighty God's power.
When one stops fighting with the inevitable,
One creates new energy to face that inevitable.

Bend like the willow; don't resist like the oak,
This is a reality which many wise men spoke.
What can't be cured must be endured is the rule divine,
When you can do nothing, why do you mind.

Life is an index of our inner thoughts,
Happiness or misery is felt due to those thoughts.
One feels happy with positive attitude,
One feels sad with negative attitude.

100. Going Going Gone is The Rule of The World

Let by gone be by gone,
Don't repent why it had gone.
Going, going, gone is the rule of the world,
None can change this rule of the world.

Why do you worry about your past,
Everything will have to go at last.
Try to enjoy your present life,
Don't bother about the future life,

Past is dead, future is not known,
Many factors keep it always unknown.
Those who spoil their present life expecting a better future,
Can neither enjoy their present, nor their future.

Live in the present and do your best,
To the will of God try to adjust.
This is the way to enjoy the life.
This is the way to have peace in life.

What is ordained is ordained,
Only the will of God can refrain.
People blame others for all their troubles,
Try to find remedy than blaming others for troubles.

101. Forgive and Forget is The Best

If any selfish person takes any undue advantage of you,
No revenge should be taken by you.
It would be better to cross them off your list,
Rather than try to get even and hit.

If you will try to get even, you will wreck your health,
To regain that health you will also lose your wealth.
Resentment may cause you hypertension and heart disease,
It may also encourage any psychosomatic disease.

Love your enemy, many religions so teach,
To provide you peace of mind, they so preach.
It can help to avoid ulcer, high BP, and heart troubles,
Can protect you from many other troubles.

Hatred destroys our ability to digest our food,
Such type of people always brood.
If you want to lead a happy and calm life,
Then don't permit your enemy to poke nose in your life.

If you don't like to love your enemy,
Then atleast forgive and forget your enemy.
None can humiliate or disturb any person,
Unless it is the desire of that person.

When anybody abuses you; you angrily react,
If you just laugh away; then the abusers have to retract.

102. Don't Expect Gratitude

Don't expect gratitude for your every act,
Don't bother if you do not get your due respect.
It is natural for the people to forget gratitude,
Then why do you expect from them any gratitude.

An ideal person takes joy in doing favours for others,
But never expect gratitude from the others.
You should give only for the inner joy of giving,
Then you will start feeling a strange happy living.

Don't become excited if you receive gratitude,
Don't feel sad if you do not receive gratitude.
If you want happiness never expect gratitude,
Give for the joy of giving and not for any gratitude.

If you want to make your children grateful,
You will have to make yourself grateful.
Don't try to belittle others before your children,
It will cultivate ungratefulness in your children.

Selfishness, egotism and ungratefulness are common traits,
The world is full of the people with such traits.
To do something to get gratitude is a selfishness of strange kind,
Selfish thinking always affects our heart and mind.

103. Why Don't You Think and Thank

More than ninety percent things are always right,
Less than ten percent things may not be right.
Those who want peace of mind concentrate on right things,
Those who do not want peace concentrate on wrong things.

Think of all those things we have to be grateful,
For all our boons and bounties, we must be graceful.
People never think of what they have,
They always think of what they do not have.

Would you like to sell both your eyes at any price?
Would you like to sell both your hands and legs at any price?
God has provided us many boons and bounties,
But we never thank God for those boons and bounties.

You are not the only person full of troubles,
The world is full of people with many troubles.
If you will go on growling and grumbling,
You will lose your health and happiness due to that grumbling.

Many people are suffering more than you,
Why not this thought gives consolation to you.
Count your blessings and not your troubles,
To enjoy peace of mind prick the bubble.

Many people often worry themselves about the things that rarely happen,
But never bother to know, why that will happen.
Due to worries of misfortunes, they always feel bitter,
They should also know the law of average to wipe out their jitter.

For one thing or the other some people always feel worried,
They can pick up any problem to become worried.

104. You Are The Only One in The Whole World

You are the one and only one in the whole world,
You can't be compared with anyone else in the whole world.
Don't try to fit yourself into a pattern which is not your own,
Don't try to imitate mode of life of others which is not your own.

Remain yourself, what you really are.
Try to find out what really you are.
Every person has some hidden specific qualities,
Find out and try to develop all those qualities.

You feel miserable, when try to become somebody,
Something other than the person in your own body.
What you are not, don't pretend to be,
By imitating a lion, you can't a lion be.

No body ever wants a counterfeit coin,
You must try to show real value of your coin.
An average person develops about ten percent of his latent abilities,
They fail to utilise all their hidden capabilities.

Neither there was any other person exactly like you,
Nor there would be any other person exactly like you.
Make the most of what nature has provided you,
You are what your heredity, experience and environment had made you.

Envy is ignorance and imitation is suicide,
Whatever you have, accept that with pride.

Neither you can know what you want, nor can know yourself,
Until you are willing to become your own self.

No one can be any one else, without harming own personality,
Copying others can deprive you of developing your own personality.
By copying others you can easily earn a lot of money,
But not the satisfaction which is more valuable than money.

105. You Are Not The Biggest

Glow worms think they are only lighting up the world,
Their vanity passes away when stars appear and lighting up the world.
Their vanity also passes away when the moon appears and lights up,
All become visible when the sun appears and lights up.
O rich man ! you must ponder over these natural facts,
Some body might be richer than you, it is a fact.

106. Spit Out Your Worries

When we frankly talk with someone about our worries,
We feel instant relief from our worries,
It is like spitting out our worries,
Or getting it off our chest all those worries.

Find any reliable person with whom you may talk,
You will feel relief from inner anxieties after that talk.
By talking, one gains better insight about the troubles,
And get a better perspective of those troubles.

Develop a friendly interest in the people who share your life,
You will be escaped from boredom in your life.
Prayer also acts like sharing worries with God,
One feels relaxed after praying to God.

Find any appropriate person to talk about your worries,
Vomit before him all your inner worries.
You will feel relief in your mind,
It is a solution to get some peace of mind.

Attending religious meetings is also useful,
Worried people can exchange their worries and become hopeful.
Social gatherings also provide an appropriate platform,
To exchange our worries at that platform.

107. Prayer Can Do Wonders

Prayer is the most powerful form of energy,
Like Radium it also produces luminous and self generating energy.
When one prays one links itself with the inexhaustible motive power,
Universe is being run by that power.

We seek to augment that finite energy,
By addressing ourselves to that finite source of energy.
Whenever we address God in fervent prayer,
Our body and mind feel better after that prayer.

Only faith and God can help us to utilize our hidden energy,
Without his inspiration none can awaken that energy.
Prayer can help all types of persons,
One may be a theist or an atheist person.

When all types of therapy had badly failed,
Through sincere prayers any body can hail.
Prayer helps to put into words what is troubling our mind,
It is like understanding the problem that is hurting our mind.

One can discuss with God even the most secret problems,
And can feel relaxed after sharing those problems.
Prayer encourages us to take some actions,
Then we feel peace as a reaction.

Pent up energy releases, when one says prayer,
Incurable diseases can be cured with the prayer.
That is why all the religions greatly emphasize to say regular prayer,
Panacea for many troubles is the sincere prayer.

Don't say your prayers just as a formality,
Pray from the core of your heart, not as a formality.

108. Boredom Causes Fatigue

Boredom is the main cause of our fatigue,
Physical work does not cause very much fatigue.
If the work is interesting we don't feel fatigue,
If we have no interest in the work, we start feeling fatigue.

Our emotional attitude is the main cause of our fatigue,
Physical exertion produces very little fatigue.
In boredom our BP rises and consumption of oxygen decreases,
We start feeling eye-strain, headache and our tiredness increases.

One rarely feels tired while doing something interesting and
        exciting,
That is why for many long hours a writer goes on writing.
Boredom is caused when one takes no interest in work,
When the work is interesting, workers can do more work.

Fatigue is not caused by doing any work,
But by worry, frustration and resentment caused by that work.
With a nagging wife you can't walk even one hundred meters,
With your sweetheart, you can walk easily many kilometers.

Even if your work is not interesting, do acting that the work is
        interesting,
Acting can tend to make your work really interesting.
If in your work you don't find happiness,
In your real life also you can't find happiness.

By getting interested in job will save you from worries,
As it will take your mind off your worries.
It will also reduce fatigue in your mind,
And may help you to enjoy peace of mind.

109. How To Achieve Happy Family Life

Every person wants to lead a happy family life,
But many factors are there that sour the happy life.
Nagging and scolding accomplish nothing in life,
But can be a cause of any tragedy in a happy life.

Nagging and scolding is a devastating force,
It can wreck a happy life with great force.
Never criticize each other or say any word of reproach,
Try to win the heart, which is a good approach.

Success in marriage does not depend on just choosing the right person,
It mainly depends on being the right person.
Those who try to make their partner over,
Always repent afterwards when the time is over.

Rant and rave never help any body,
These only bring misery to everybody.
Many have a peculiar habit of finding fault with others,
Never bother to think how they are hurting the others.

Appreciate your partner in a sincere and honest way,
To lead a happy life it is an easiest way.
Women attach importance to birthdays and anniversaries,
Don't forget your wife's birthday and marriage anniversary.

Even one trivial incidence can wreck a happy family life,
Learn to overlook them to lead a happy life.
Courtesy plays an important role in married life,
As oil plays an important role in a machine's life.

Sexual ignorance is also a cause of divorce,
Why not read any good book on sex to avoid such a divorce.
Sex is the main satisfaction in a married life,
A dissatisfied couple can wreck their happy family life.

Marital quarrels can cause you ulcer, haedache and pain,
As these keep the nervous system always in strain.
Never go to bed angry with your wife,
Try to live a quiet and serene life.

110. Real Bliss

Real bliss is being guarded by a five hooded serpent,
Our own mind itself is that five hooded serpent.
It hisses through its five senses to divert our attention,
From the real bliss it keeps away our attention.
None can attain real happiness without taming that serpent,
Lord Krishna was able to tame that serpent.

111. Hurdles

Passions are a hurdle between soul and God,
When these are removed, soul moves towards the God.
Rampant materialism has distorted the life,
One never thinks beyond comforts and family life.

112. Your Attitude Can Make or Mar Your Life

Your happiness depends upon your attitude to life,
Your attitude may make or mar your life.
Negative attitude brings pain and sorrow in life,
Positive attitude is the source of goodness in life.

But attitude is not a rigid mental condition,
One can change from negative to positive mental condition.
You can control your attitude with definiteness of purpose,
Get rid of fears and doubts when you are sure about your purpose.

Your mind will be focused on that purpose,
Then mind will not get astray from that purpose.
When mind is concentrated, success is sure,
Holymen also use this technique to make themselves ensure.

Then all efforts are lined up to help to attain that purpose,
The person won't feel discouraged from obstacles to achieve that
          purpose.
Many successful persons are not very intelligent in mind,
But have the ability to concentrate the mind.

Their positive attitude ensures them all the success,
They know that positive attitude is the philosophy of success.
A positive mind gets benefits from other positive minds,
Imagined obstacles disappear from a positive mind.

When you send your positive thoughts to other minds,
You receive back kindered thoughts from those minds.
When you start doubting anybody in your mind,
You cannot get any benefit from that mind.

113. Transmutation of Sex Can Change Your Destiny

Animals and plants do sex activities only in a certain season,
But men and women do it in every season.
That is why sex is causing many troubles for many people,
They think God made the sex to be enjoyed by the people.

Sex can take the man away from God, some think so,
To escape from its fury and ecstasy, they renounce the world to lay low.
If properly transmuted, sex can change the destiny of the person,
It is a great creative force which is found in every person.

When this energy is focused into other channels in life,
It tremendously increases one's power of achievement in life.
It does not mean lessening one's sex energy,
But shifting it to other uses of that energy.

Sex energy is like a power-house of life,
It can be transmuted to any sphere of life.
Sexual thoughts often greatly disturb the mind,
Which devoids the person to concentrate the mind.

Focussing of inward forces is a must to achieve success in life,
A wandering mind often hinders the progress in life.
The desire for physical contact is diverted towards science or art,
Then it plays a very important and specific part.

But it does not interfere with the natural sex act,
When it is transmuted, no desire is left for physical contact.
Sooner you find this secret, longer you will enjoy life,
But it depends upon your own experiences in life.

Sex can make or mar the human life,
It depends upon how one uses it in real life.
Most of the people believe in the maximum enjoyment of sex,
But holymen believe in controlling and transmuting the sex.

Sex energy is a great creative faculty in life,
When properly transmuted can change the course of your life.

114. Don't Move Towards Slow Suicide

Those who don't know how to relax are committing slow suicide,
Their nervous system may break down from any side.
Life has become very fast in these days,
Many people are always in a hurry and worry in these days.

They are heavily taxing their entire nervous system,
Only relaxation can soothe the tired nervous system.
Keep yourself free from nervous fatigue and worry,
Try to avoid unnecessary hurry and worry.

Some people are always fast in their daily activities,
They get up fast and work fast in all their activities.
People often give in to the situation instead of facing it,
They try to run away from life instead of living it.

Such people ruin themselves and their family life,
Can not enjoy the peace of mind in their life.

115. God is One and Only One You Must Understand

You were born a boy or a girl, not a man of religion,
You were made to believe yourself man of any religion.
When he was born the nurse said, "A boy is born".
When she was born the nurse said, "A girl is born".

Your parents labelled you in the religion of their own,
That is why many kinds of religions are known.
Religions were made, to tell the people, how to worship God,
Religions were made, to tell the people, have faith in God.

Religions were made, to tell the people, how to make amends,
But people are using religions, to meet their selfish ends.
Many wars and battles were fought, in the name of religion,
Many people were butchered and maimed, in the name of religion.

Many people are being exploited, in the name of religion,
Many people are being befooled, in the name of religion.
Religions teach us, love mankind, not to hate and fight,
Religions teach us, help the poors, not to exploit their rights.

Religions teach us, make the society useful and bright,
Religions teach us, shun violence always be polite.
Different religions are different ways, to worship the same God,
By hating any other religion you are insulting your own God.

Religion is a private matter, why not take this stand,
To save the people from brutal killings on this very land.
God lives in his creations on this very land,
First God is your mother, then your motherland.

Your work is also worship you must understand,
To shirk work is a treachery of the motherland.
To help the poor and helpless is true worship on land,
This is the only universal religion, you must understand.

You were born a boy or a girl not a man of religion.
You were made to believe yourself man of any religion.

116. Rama Krishna Says

There should be harmony between your thoughts and speech,
Only then your message in the heart of others can reach.
Those who are simple can attain the God,
Thief of their own thoughts can't attain the God.
One who does any thing only for sake of show,
He is very cunning person very very low.

117. Pain

Humans find themselves always in pain,
But don't know the real cause of their pain.
Right belief, right thoughts, right meditation,
Right speech, right action and right dedication.
Means of livelihood should also be right,
Energy that one gets should also be right.

From Brihadarnyakopanishad
118. The Verse of The Honey

Let the air blow honey,
Let the rivers pour honey.
Let the plants be sweet with honey,
Let the days and nights be filled with honey.

Let the dust of the earth be sprinkled with honey,
May our forefathers in heaven be of honey.
May the trees be full of honey,
May the sunrays bring honey.

A Message From *Brihadarñyakopanishad*

(Brihadarñyakopanishad is a collection of many stories and theories regarding not only Brahma but also other aspects of life. Some of the passages are similar with other Upanishads. Yajañvalkya was the main figure of this Upanishad. It is the largest Upanishad and forms a part of the ShatPath Brahmana of the White Yajurveda. A talk between Yajañvalkya and his wife Maitreyi is regarded as a landmark in the propagation of the ideas of Upanishads.)

119. Who Bothers For Heaven?

Humans are very happy in their present form,
Don't want to leave it in which they are born.
Once Goddess Laxmi saw a pig rolling in the mire,
Was eating rubbish which he admired.

Laxmi felt sad at his plight,
Wanted to set his condition quite right.
Complained God Vishnu against that injustice,
Made a request to give him justice.

He should also be brought to heaven,
To enjoy life in their heaven.

*Vishnu—   *"I never desired that he should stink in the mire,*
          But to leave that mire he has no desire.
          He feels very happy in that mire,
          I can do nothing against his desire."

+Laxmi—   *"I do not agree with you on this point.*
          Who does not want heaven, is the main point.
          All sensible persons want to live in heaven,
          It is not possible to refuse heaven."

Narad was sent to bring the pig to heaven,
To persuade him to come to heaven.
Narad gave him the message of Lord Vishnu,
Requested him to get ready to meet Lord Vishnu.

Pig—   *"Who is God Vishnu, I don't know.*
        What is that heaven, I don't want to know.

---

* God of Protection
+ Goddess of Wealth.

I am very happy with family and wife,
In this quagmire I am enjoying my life.

Please don't disturb me, go from here.
Let me and wife enjoy life here.
Everything is Okay here, for me.
Many kinds of comforts are available to me."

*Narad—   "Why are you suffering in this mire,
It is the most dirty place whom you admire.
You will drink nectar in that heaven,
Will become immortal in that heaven."

Pig—   "All kinds of comforts are available here,
What more can you give me there?
I don't understand what you advise,
Let me consult wife to have her advice."

He told his wife about the man of Vishnu,
Who wanted to take them to Lord Vishnu.
He says, "We will be very happy there,
Everything in plenty is available there".

Wife—   "You see, I am now in the family way,
Will give birth to the babies in a few days.
Then we will marry our sons and daughters,
They will also have their own sons and daughters.

They will call us grandfather and mother,
We will feel proud in relatives and brothers,
We don't want to sacrifice, enjoyment of life,
Which we are enjoying as husband and wife.

---

* Saint, son of Lord Brahma.

119

We acquired this estate after great sacrifice,
Don't want to leave it at any price.
In our circle we have a name,
After many struggles, have earned this fame.

Please go back and tell your Vishnu,
We are not interested in heaven of Vishnu.
We are quite satisfied in this life,
Don't want to abandon it at any price."

120. Lust

Mind remains irritated due to sensual pleasure,
Mind refuses to leave completely the sensual pleasure.
Desires may be suppressed only for a short time,
Desires arise again and again in our mind.

Lust for sex, wealth and money is difficult to hold,
With every enjoyment goes on increasing many fold.
Lust, anger and greed always obstruct peace of mind,
Try to control them to obtain peace of mind.

121. Sex Urge is a Mighty Force

Reproductive urge plays a very important role in life,
May be the husband or the wife.
It is very mighty force difficult to escape,
Even many holy people are not able to escape.

It helps in the development of culture and talent,
To gifted people it provides more and more talent.
No sphere of human activity is immune from sex urge,
Even religion are full of disguised sex urge.

Literary and dramatic output revolves around this urge,
The world of entertainment is also built around this urge.
Our dreams are also a hunting ground for the sexual urge,
The most important topic for all ages is the sexual urge.

It has a very powerful effect, on our thoughts in whole life,
Starts from puberty and ends with the end of the life.
Nature has planted this urge so deep in human life,
Very difficult to negate it by any human in life.

Those who try to negate or suppress it in any way,
Have to pay a heavy price come what may.
It can't be suppressed but one can transmute,
To utilize this power to produce more attribute.

Yogies utilise this power to gain spirituality,
Its normal use is a hindrance to progress in spirituality.

122. A Talk Between Yajañvalkya and His Wife Maitreyi

Yajanvalkya had Katyani and Maitreyi, two lovely wives,
Katyani was worldly, while Maitreyi was spiritually wise.
When Yajanvalkya decided to renounce the world,
To acquire true knowledge of the world.

He approached his wife Maitreyi for her consent,
And to divide his wealth between both, with their mutual consent,
But Maitreyi refused to accept any wealth,
Because immortality cannot be gained with the wealth.

O dear husband! if you really love me,
Whatever you know about Brahma please tell me.
O dear Maitreyi! you were always very dear to me,
Your question is also a favourite of me.

Please listen to me with attentive mind,
And try to understand it with your mind.
A husband is not dear for the sake of husband but for one's own self,
A wife is not dear for the sake of wife but for one's own self.

A son is not dear for son's sake but for the sake of the self,
Wealth is not dear for the sake of wealth but for the own self.
All are dear not for all but for the sake of the self,
Everybody likes to satisfy one's own self.

Therefore self should be seen, heard and contemplated upon,
Self is very dear to us, so it should be meditated upon.
When one plays any musical instrument,
Ears grasp only one tune of different tunes of that instrument.

After inner knowledge all sounds seem to give one tune,
Ears of the mind then listen only one tune.
After appropriate knowledge Brahma can be felt everywhere,
As dissolved salt can't be seen but may be felt in water everywhere.

It is out of atma (soul) that everything else springs,
In him everything lives and everything dissolves in him.
When the senses feel duality in our mind,
Only then one can see, smell, hear and speak of other kinds.

But when the self merges into the soul and becomes one,
All the duality ceases and one becomes only one.
Existence of the world can't be known without atma (soul),
To explain the existence of the world it is a must to know atma.

As smoke gives indication of the existence of fire,
No smoke is possible without the fire.
Similarly world is an indication of the existence of Brahma,
There might be any creator of this world, who is none else but Brahma.

When the world is dissolved by Brahma,
Everything dissolves except the consciousness of Brahma.
In this life you are subject to hunger, thirst, birth and death,
After knowing you will dissolve into Brahma who is without
                    fear of birth and death.

Consciousness that is born out of Avidya (ignorance),
Of the complex of body, senses and mind is destroyed with Vidya.
Brahma is the Atma of all beings,
And does not perish with the perish of all beings.

123. What To Eat, What Not To Eat

What to eat, what not to eat, all religions preach,
How to eat and when to eat, this they also teach.
Beef is forbidden in the Hindu religion,
But it is allowed in many other religions.

Pork is forbidden in the Muslim religion,
But it is gladly eaten in many other religions.
A true Muslim never touches pork and wine,
Some religions allow it and never mind.

Hindu religion is very strict about the food we eat,
Because as we eat, so our mind treats.
It recommends Satvik and vegetarian diet,
Even forbids onion, garlic, chilly in diet.

These kinds of foods greatly irritate the mind,
Devoid concentration and distract the mind.
Vegetarian is cheaper than non-vegetarian diet,
Makes the mind less aggressive than the other diets.

Religious followers think their religion is better than the others,
Blindly follow religious instructions, don't listen to others.

124. AIDS

Dope and sex are not enjoyment but the biggest weakness,
It is not a real enjoyment but a mental weakness.
History had repeated itself a number of times,
Many rolled in the dust due to drugs, sex and wine.

Then why people become mad in this mad race,
To get some enjoyment they forget all grace,
Why dope, sex and wine is your biggest weakness.
Drugs, sex and liquor are the cause of many corruptions.

Why not nip this evil in the bud then.
After giving momentary pleasure always leave in the lurch,
To find out some real enjoyment why not make some search.
Lust for the sex is your biggest weakness.

Misuse of sex is the main cause of AIDS,
After making it free for all now you feel afraid.
Sex is a reproductive power not a thing for trade,
Don't use it like a weapon in business or trade.

To satisfy sex at any cost is your biggest weakness.
Sex and AIDS are best friends always keep in mind,
Never do sex with a stranger, I want to remind.
As you sow, so will reap, is the rule divine,

Keep a check on sex abuses and have peace of mind,
Pursuit of pleasure is your biggest weakness.

125. O Drug Addict You are Playing With The Fire

O, dope addict you are playing with the fire,
Playing with the fire, dear playing with the fire.
Taking drugs is like playing with the fire,
Consequences always are very very dire.

You are losing your health and wealth,
And are moving to the valley of death.

Drugs only take to the fool's paradise,
Why have you become so unwise?
Your family is also facing the ire,
It is a death knell, why playing with this fire,

All the drugs are like a cobra,
And poison the body like a cobra.
May it be marijuana, smack or cocaine,
Opium or heroin or morphine,

Wake up, wake up, from this slumber, why losing your health,
It will surely devoid you from your wealth.
It is not difficult to come out from its spell,
Why are you taking them? You understand well.

These are taking you towards the pyre,
O drug addict you are playing with the fire.

126. The End Result of The Wealth

Those for whom I sacrificed whole youthful life,
Are eagerly awaiting the end of my life.
After borrowing from here and there, I made a home for them,
I used to lead a very simple life to give comforts to them.

To make them well settled, I worked day and night,
Now they are very eager to see my death in sight.
My wealth has become a bone of contention,
All my darlings have very bad intention.

They have selfish motives, I don't want to mention,
Secretly they are planning to get hold of my mansion.
I never thought one day I would also be old,
But I am now old, I am now old.

127. Money is Very Thankless

People take many troubles to earn more and more money,
As it seems to them more sweet than honey.
They expect from it luxuries and comforts in life,
Respect from kinsmen, children and wife.

But it is very thankless only heart burning breeds,
Produces discontentment, avarice and greed.
Is very fickle never gives ease,
Produces many mental and physical diseases.

128. A Message From Dhammapad* on Buddhism

Do good deeds and sow good seeds,
Evil deeds evil breed.
When you make anybody happy, happiness you sow,
When you make anybody unhappy, unhappiness you sow.

When you do cruel things, you sow cruelty,
Afterwards it grows up into cruelty.
When you do kindness, kindness you sow,
When you do cheating, cheating you grow.

When you yourself don't like death or to suffer pain,
Why are you giving to others death or pain.
Whatever you sow, so you reap,
Good or bad you yourself heap.

Desires breed misery you must understand,
Keep them in check if you can.

Rust
Rust and evil deeds do the same action,
One eats the iron, other eats the body as a reaction.
To save the iron from the rust some paint is needed,
To save the body from the rust good deeds are needed.

Death
One who is born must have to die,
Birth is certain for those who have died,
Cycle of birth and death is inevitable,
Only God has the power to make it alterable.

---
* An ancient Buddhist Monk.

129. Lust, Anger and Greed are The Gates To the Hell

Lust, anger and greed are the gates to the Hell,
It has been told in the Gita very well.
These are the enemies of peace of mind,
And are the masters in disturbing the mind.

Egoism is the root cause of our anger,
Many evils take their origin in our anger.
It has the power to destroy peace of mind,
It can very easily confuse the mind.

An angry person does not know what he is going to do.
Even murder or fight he can easily do.
When a man's desire is not gratified,
He becomes angry and terrified.

Resentment, indignation, wrath and irritation,
Annoyance, fury and rage produce provocation.
Transmutation of anger can produce strange energy,
One can move the world with that energy.

Anger is a poison that spoils the blood,
By adding various poisonous substances in the blood.
Many diseases are caused due to anger,
Rheumatic, heart and nervous diseases are caused by the anger.

Even one fit of anger can shatter the entire nervous system,
Then it takes many months to restore that damaged nervous system.
Love, forgiveness and compassion can defeat the anger,
Why not try them to control your anger.

130. Greed

Greed and anger are the intimate friends,
Avarice and covetousness are also good friends.
A greedy man has attachment only for his money,
His blood and life is only the money.

Greed always makes the mind restless,
Avarice also makes the mind to feel restless.
A greedy person is never satisfied even with a million,
After million always thinks how to change that into a billion.

A greedy person always feels disturbed in his mind,
And can't find the peace of mind.
Always tries to get more and more,
Until he remains in the world no more.

131. Improve Your Worldly Wisdom Through *Hitopodesha*

Hitopodesha is the most popular and famous Sanskrit book which had already inspired and is still inspiring many people. It had been translated in many languages of the world. Everything is explained through comprehensive and simple animal stories. The listeners are expected to grasp the moral of the story themselves. It is one of the oldest methods of teaching when textbooks were not available. The hand-written books were used to teach the children of the kings, nobles and rich families. It was a story-telling method. After telling the story, the moral was wound up in a Sanskrit shloka. The students were expected to learn that shloka by heart.

I have translated main ideas of a few of those shlokas into English Couplets. I am sure readers will enjoy it and may like to read it again and again. All the couplets are full of worldly knowledge and wisdom to become a wise person in the society. All the couplets directly touch our heart as those are related to real life situations of our day to day life.

1.
What is the advantage of eyes to a blind man,
What is the advantage of a foolish son to a wise man.

2.
A son unborn or dead causes grief for a short time,
But a foolish son causes grief for a long time.

3.
One wise son is better than one hundred foolish sons,
To remove the darkness there is only one Sun.

4.

Health, wealth, loving wife and obedient children,
These gifts of God are available only to a few ones.

5.

Attachment to money and life is strong in human life,
But to an old man his young wife is more dear than his own
        life.

6.

People use sweet words when there is any motive,
A young wife hugs her old husband when there is any motive.

7.

In indigestion food works as a poison to a man,
A young wife also proves a poison to an old man.

8.

Eating, sleeping, fear, offsprings are common in all living things,
Only moral goodness distinguishes human from other living things.

9.

Life, action, wealth, wisdom and then death,
Is the human destiny from birth to death.

10.

Lazy people believe in fate while wise believe in action,
Where there is an action, there is surely a reaction.

11.

In fine clothes every person appears a gentle person,
Only the speech reveals, of what type is that person.

12.

Avarice can make even a wise person blind,
Although they can see yet not from their mind.

13.

In adversities, mind also becomes very smear,
Even Lord Rama believed in the existence of a golden deer.

14.

One who praises at the face, but abuses at the back,
Is not fit for friendship, as good qualities lack.

15.

Sweet words and pretended services are used to cheat,
These tools are often used by all the cheats.

16.

Friendship should be avoided with the evil nature,
Coal may be hot or cold spoils the hand as per its nature.

17.

Many people flatter at the face but backbite at behind,
When they find any weak point, in harming they never mind.

18.

When an evil natured person speaks kindly, have no confidence
*   in him,*
His heart is full of poison upto the brim.

19.

Vices get punishment and virtues get reward,
Sooner or later everybody gets its due award.

20.
A woman is like butter, a man is like fire,
It is not wise to put the butter close to the fire.

21.
Poverty and death both give pain,
Pain of death is shortlived, but pain of poverty always remains.

22.
It is money which is respected not the person who holds,
As soon as one loses the money, is ignored like an old.

23.
Poverty destroys virtues, old age destroys beauty,
Sunlight destroys darkness, servitude destroys sense of duty.

24.
Food at the expense of others, love bought for money,
These are the miseries, never give a taste like honey.

25.
Delight in poetry, company of virtues in the world,
Are the two sweet fruits on the poisonous tree of the world.

26.
One who hoards money at the cost of happiness,
Neither enjoys money, nor gets happiness.

27.
A miser's life is just like a blacksmith's bellow,
Although he is breathing, yet a wretched fellow.

28.

As a lamp shows nothing to a blind man,
Scriptures have no value for a foolish man.

29.

Pain and pleasure are like two wheels,
Without them our life can not reel.

30.

Even without riches a wise man gains honour,
But even with riches a miser gains dishonour.

31.

Youth, riches, parents and beauty,
Abandon everybody after doing their duty.

32.

Fortunes never favour a lazy slack man,
As a young girl never likes to hug an old man.

33.

Sex, bad health, home sickness and idleness,
Are a few obstacles in the way of greatness.

34.

Appearance, movement, eyes, speech, gestures and gait,
What is in the mind, can clearly indicate.

35.

A crow takes nothing, a cuckoo gives nothing,
Sweet words get appreciation and harsh words get nothing.

36.

For fear of indigestion, none will like to eat nothing,
From fear of mistakes, why do you like to do nothing.

37.

A creeper itself winds around whatever is nearby,
A minister shows favour to the person who is nearby.

38.

Weapon, book, lute, speech of any person,
Their usefulness depends on the use by the person.

39.

A corrupt mind always thinks about evil things,
Shakuni and Shaktare are the proofs of this thing.

40.

Power and riches change every mind,
The owner misconceives that he has a very great mind.

41.

Affections of a wicked person can not be gained,
As from a poisonous tree good fruit can not be obtained.

42.

Secret confidence is like the seed of a plant,
If one breaks it, it can't be used to implant.

43.

An angry person may be pacified, if causes of anger are removed,
But a person with hostile mind, can not be moved.

44.

To meet their selfish ends, scounderals corrupt a virtuous man,
This is the easiest method used by a wicked man.

45.

Mere knowledge of a medicine can't cure disease,
Proper diagnose is a must to eradicate that disease.

46.

A crow is very clever but eats filthy things,
A clever person always miseries brings.

47.

Learning is that eye which clears many doubts,
Reveals many hidden things without any doubt.

48.

Lazy people believe only in their fate,
Diligent neither shirk work nor they hate.

49.

Result of the past deeds is called fate,
So why not work with vigour to make your fate.

50.

To give birth to a son can't make the son wise,
Proper guidance only can make him wise.

51.

Sloth, slumber, fear, anger and postponement,
Are the main obstacles in the way of attainment.

52.

With heavy make-up and fine clothes every woman looks pretty,
Only her speech reveals about the type of her beauty.

53.

A frog is never attracted to the lotus, though living nearby,
But a bee runs towards the lotus, though not living nearby.

54.

A virtuous person appreciates virtues in others,
A person who is not good in himself, never cares for others.

55.

When a person of lower mind is raised to an honourable post,
Tries to get rid of that person, who helped him to get that post.

56.

The parents who fail to give proper education to their children,
Are the worst enemies of their own children.

57.

Avarice is the cause of many misdeeds,
It is the root of many evils, one must take heed.

58.

Cheerfulness in adversity and calmness in prosperity,
Are rarely seen in the humanity.

59.

A dog that has lost teeth, licks a bone to have some taste.
A helpless old person also likes to enjoy senses to have their taste.

60.

Likeness or dislikeness depends upon enjoymet,
As cattle like to wander anywhere in search of enjoyment.

61.

Some women remain unfaithful even among Gods,
Those are very lucky, whose wives are faithful to their lords.

62.

A person should conceal age, money, penance and medicine he
       takes,
Domestic troubles, private counsels, liberality and his disgrace.

63.

Poverty is the root of many evils in the world,
It makes the person to lose self respect in this world.

64.

It is better to remain silent than speaking unkind words,
Better to be impotent than philandering in the world.

65.

A covetous person never heeds any kind of reason,
Greed always compels not to listen to good reasons.

66.

A greedy person can never be made contented,
Even after getting whole world's wealth, remains discontented.

67.

It is not the money that makes one rich,
It is the contentment that makes one rich.

68.

Those who acquire ill-gotten money can't get peace,
It is the contentment that gives peace.

69.

To get something, a greedy man can travel for many miles,
But a contented person doesn't bother for undue things, even lying
nearby.

70.

Discrimination between good and bad is the real learning,
Money earned through righteous means is the real earning.

71.

Compassion towards all is the real happiness,
Freedom from diseases is the real happiness.

72.

What is the use of money, not given or used,
What is the use of scriptures whose teachings are not used.

73.

A miser's wealth is nothing more, than a piece of stone,
Either it is destroyed or taken away by the persons unknown.

74.

Liberality with kindness, contempt for illegal wealth of all kinds,
Bravery with forbearance, knowledge with pride,
These are the good qualities, very difficult to find.

75.

The mere name of a drug can't cure disease,
Knowledge without action always cease.

76.

Heaping of the riches gives troubles and not happiness,
Loss of the riches gives sorrow, then how riches can give happiness.

77.

Keep away from mud than to wash it off,
Keep away from ill-gotten wealth than to pass it off.

78.

A rich man is afraid of fire, thieves, rulers, relatives and all beings,
As there is a danger of death to all living beings.

79.

Wealth is difficult to acquire and very difficult to keep,
Its loss is very painful, be careful when wealth you seek.

80.

To visit without invitation, to speak without being asked,
To think oneself valuable to one's master is a foolish task.

81.

Mind your own business is a good advice,
Before meddling in anyone's affairs think it thrice.

82.

Success or failure are the ways of life,
Bear them happily to lead a happy life.

83.

Incapacity causes misfortunes, expedient causes prosperity,
A wise person can change his adversity into prosperity.

84.

One can wear a piece of glass on hand, and on foot can wear a jewel,
But as value is concerned, a glass is a glass and a jewel is a jewel.

85.

One who is respected by the ruler is respected by all,
Degraded by the ruler is despised by all.

86.

If one can't overpower an insignificant enemy,
Put forward an opponent to seize that enemy.

87.

The hurricane never hurts grass, which is not mighty,
It uproots only lofty trees, as a mighty fights a mighty.

88.

A squanderer loses everything after some time,
May be holding billions at a particular time.

89.

Wood can't satisfy the fire, rivers can't satisfy the ocean,
Beauty can't be satisfied after millions of adorations.

90.

One who does not lose heart at unexpected events,
Can easily win over all such events.

91.

As poisonous herbs and loose teeth are quickly removed,
Evil minister should also be quickly removed.

92.

Everyone desires fortunes and admires beauty,
Everybody looks with longing on the young beauty.

93.

Don't punish anybody without investigation,
Information of others may prove wrong after investigation.

94.

To reward or punish without considering merits or faults,
Is like to play with a lion who may tear apart.

95.

A drowning man if lays hold of a serpent,
Can neither hold on, nor let go that serpent.

96.

Roots are full of snakes, flowers are full of bees,
Branches are full of monkeys, that is the fate of a sandal tree.

97.

To quarrel with the family, to adopt improper business,
To contend with stronger, to disclose secret of any kind,
Always leads towards a downfall, keep it in mind.

98.

A villain carries corruption wherever he goes,
Ravana carried away Sita ignoring his vow.

99.

Don't contest with anybody before knowing his strength,
Otherwise you will have to lose all your strength.

100.

Youth, beauty, life, riches, power and friends,
Pass away quickly without any amends.

101.

Fear from the danger when it is at a distance,
Face it bravely, when not at a distance.

102.

As the same person forms many relations in this world,
So, many thorns of sorrow he plants in this world.

103.

Receive a friend with kindness, a relative with affectionate haste,
Servants and women with gifts and honour without being late.

132. How One Desire Breeds Another Desire?

A holyman made a hut to do meditation,
To do yoga and recitation.
As his guru advised him he renounced everything,
He wore only a kopeen (underwear) and denounced other things.

After taking a bath he hanged his kopeen to dry,
To get food, he used to go to the village nearby.
One day when he returned he found holes in his underwear,
Which were made by the rats that lived near.

He had to go to the village for a fresh one,
But all were spoiled whenever he hanged any one.
Villagers were unwilling to supply him kopeen again and again,
They requested him to keep a cat, when he went there again.

A cat will surely keep away the rats,
The rats always feel afraid of the cat.
The sadhu brought the cat into his hut,
The rats never dared again to enter into the hut.

He fed the cat with the milk of the villagers,
But it was not possible to get milk daily from the villagers.
The villagers again requested him to keep a cow,
To feed the cat and himself with the milk of that cow.

They provided him a nice milch cow,
Now there was a problem of fodder for that cow.
The villagers suggested him to cultivate an uncultivated piece of land.
The sadhu at once started tilling that land.

It saved him from begging for himself and the cow,
He easily got food from the land and milk from the cow.
But farming was not possible only with two hands,
He needed someone as a helping hand.

Now he engaged a labourer as a helping hand,
To look after the cow and the produce of the land.
He passed his days like a busy house-holder,
Had to do all the works of a house-holder.

When his guru again came back there,
Was very puzzled when he could not find him there.
He enquired from the servant about the fate of the sadhu,
But the servant was ignorant about any sadhu.

In the meantime the sadhu came out from his home,
And took his guru inside the home.
Guru enquired from him how all that happened,
Why was he doing cultivation instead of meditation?

He told his guru about all his curries,
How for the sake of a kopeen, he accepted all these worries.
The desire of a cloth entirely changed his life,
From an ascetic, he adopted again a worldly life.

He had to gather many kinds of goods and chattles,
That made his life very much rattle.
Desires always chain a person into the bondage,
Desist from desires to free yourself from that bondage.

A person with minimum desires is maximum happy,
A person with maximum desires can't be happy.
These are the teachings of all the holymen,
One desire breeds another desire in the minds of the men.

133. What is Special in *Bhagavad Gita*

The Gita is the knowledge of Almighty Power,
Krishna gave to Arjuna in difficult hours.
It is the science of the Absolute God,
Scripture of the Yoga to find that God.

It is a part of the battle of Mahabharat,
Kauravas Pandavas fought this battle of Mahabharat.
Wise men never grieve for the dead or alive,
Thou remained and will remain in any life.

The souls go on changing from one to another form,
Existent will not cease; non-existent will not born.
As a person casts off worn out clothes,
Puts on new clothes discarding old clothes.

Souls also cast off worn out bodies,
And again enter in new bodies.
Water, weapon, wind, fire can't cleave the soul,
Uncleavable and eternal is the soul.

It is all pervading, fire can't burn it,
Wind can't dry it, water can't wet it.
One who is born must have to die,
Birth is certain for those who have died.

Cycle of birth and death is inevitable,
Only realisation of Brahma can make it alterable.
Thou has a right only on your actions,
Thou has no right on the fruit of those actions.

Do all actions without attachment or motive,
The fruit of actions should not be thy motive.
In sorrow and pleasure if one has untroubled mind,
Passion, fear, rage have passed away from the mind.

You are like a sage of well settled mind,
Can attain the God with the control of mind.
Draw away the senses from the objects of senses,
As a tortoise withdraws his organs of senses.

Objects of senses give birth to attachment,
Desires are produced due to those attachments.
Then in turn anger and bewilderness is produced,
Destruction of intelligence is also produced.

Attachment, aversion can be controlled with the control of mind,
Then thou can control sorrows of many kinds.
Desires, longings, egoism disturb peace of mind,
Running after senses always disturbs peace of mind.

Mere control of senses without the control of mind,
Is a hypocrisy of very strange kind.
Do your work in a spirit of great sacrifice.
Perform your duty without attachment or price,

Craving and anger impell to do the sins,
Only with the wisdom you can avoid such sins.
People of doubting nature can't get happiness,
Only faith and wisdom can provide happiness.

Those who firmly believe in God,
Are only able to seek the God.

Knowledge is better than mere concentration,
But better than knowledge is the meditation.

Better than meditation is renunciation,
Peace may be gained with the renunciation.
With ill will and egoism you can't be a true devotee,
Compassion is the main sign of a true devotee.

Even minded in pain and pleasure is a true devotee,
Who has no lust, anger, greed is the true devotee.
Satav, Rajas, Tamas, Gunas are the three modes,
Goodness, passion and dullness are these modes.

Goodness produces happiness, passion produces actions,
Dullness gives ignorance as a reaction.
From goodness arises knowledge, from the passion greed,
From the dullness negligence always breeds.

When the body rises above these modes of life,
Is freed from birth and death, attains eternal life.
Satviks eat balanced food must for life,
Rajasics like tasty foods for enjoyment in life.

Tamasics like stale foods useless for life,
As per their nature they eat and drink in life.
Demonic nature has ostentation and arrogance,
Pride, anger, harshness and ignorance.

Neither they know way of action nor renunciation,
Neither purity, good conduct nor good actions.
Due to ignorance some feel they are very mighty,
Due to their wealth and power they feel they are mighty.

Due to money and muscles they believe they are powerful,
Can make anybody bow before their will.
Their only aim is to gratify their desires,
Always try to fulfil insatiable desires.

Amass hoards of wealth by unjust means,
Happily they apply all foul means.
Such people drag themselves towards the hell,
Due to bad deeds can't avoid the hell.

They take re-birth in the demonic families.
Or take birth in the lower creatures families.
Divine nature are fearless and pure in mind,
Have charity, sacrifice, austerity and control of mind.

Uprightness, non-violence, truth and forgiveness,
Tranquillity, compassion, modesty and gentleness.
Good men worship only the real Gods,
Passionate persons worship even the demi Gods.

Dull people worship spirits and ghosts,
To fulfil hidden desires they worship these ghosts.
Happiness from pure heart is the real happiness,
Objects of senses can't give the real happiness.

Sleep and sloth can't give real happiness,
Knowledge of the soul only can give real happiness.
Passions produce lust and lust produces anger,
Insatiable like fire is the lust and anger.

Lust, anger and greed are the gates to the hell,
These take the person towards the hell.

When people of demonic nature increase on the earth,
To wipe them off God descends on the earth.

To protect the nobles and punish the ignobles,
To remind values of life which are very noble.
People can worship God in any name and form,
He comes to them in the same name and form.

He never minds how you call Him,
Is ready to come in what every way you call Him.
What is now your, was with others in the past,
Why weeping you had lost nothing at last.

What you are holding will not be yours by tomorrow,
You got it from others, will go to others by morrow.
What happened or happening may be for the better,
In future also, will happen for the better.

Change is the continuous process in the world,
Going, going, gone is the rule of the world,
You brought nothing will take nothing from here,
What you have lost, was taken from here.

Pain and pleasure don't last for ever,
Only this reality will prevail for ever.
When one likes any object intimacy is produced,
Out of intimacy, desire to seek is produced.

When there is obstruction, anger is produced,
Due to that anger confusion is produced.
Due to that confusion power of reasoning is destroyed,
Then destruction of the man none can avoid.

But the man whose internal sense is under control,
Can enjoy happiness, keeping mind under control.
Senses, Mind and Reasons dwell in the body,
Can very easily confuse any body.

Mind is beyond senses, Reason is beyond Mind,
Atman (soul) is beyond reason, Senses may be controlled with the
    mind.
Who has no hate desire is the true ascetic,
Although doing Karma yet a true ascetic.

Karma Yoga and Sankhya are the similar paths,
Meet at the same spot both these paths.
Mind like wind can't be controlled,
But through practice and vairagya can be controlled.

When with practice one steadies the mind,
Through meditation even Him can find.
One who eats nothing or eats too much,
One who keeps awake or sleeps too much.

Can not succeed in attaining Yoga,
Who eats sleeps just sufficient, can attain Yoga.
Desires never satisfy by the enjoyment,
Goes on increasing after every enjoyment.

Desire is the constant enemy of the learned man,
Envelops the knowledge of the man.
Om-Tat-Sat is the root of the Universe,
By uttering these words, Brahma created Universe.

It is very simple even a child can recite,
It has immense power, you can also recite.

134. Our Heart and Blood

According to Dr. Walter B. Canon of the Harvard Medical School—Our heart pumps enough blood through our body every day. It is enough to fill a railway tank car. It exerts enough energy every twenty four hours to shovel twenty tons of coal onto a platform three feet high. It goes on doing this work upto the end of one's life. How it does?

Most people have the idea that the heart is working all the time. As a matter of fact, there is a definite rest period after each contraction. When beating at a moderate rate of seventy pulses per minute, the heart is actually working only nine hours out of the twenty-four. In the aggregate its rest periods total a full fifteen hours per day.

During meditation the heart gradually increases its period of rest.

According to Dr. Selye—In the hurry up world we are subjecting ourselves to too many stresses. We hurry constantly and worry incessantly. The businessman drives himself at his office all day, then worries half the night. The housewife tries to run her home, maintain a social life, and participate in community activities and at bed time is so jangled that she takes a sleeping pill.

Glands attempt to adjust to the continual demands of constantly increasing stress. They pour out hormones, trying to keep the body going. For a while they succeed, but in the end the defence mechanism itself breaks down. As a result, arteries harden, blood pressure rises, heart diseases develop, arthritis strikes. These and other diseases are all part of the stress picture.

Disease is caused by a chemical imbalance in the body, primarily due to stress. He bases his conclusion on the fact that the chemical balance within the body is governed mainly by three tiny glands: the pituitary and the two adrenals. The pituitary lies at the base of the brain and the two adrenals lie astride the kidneys. Their principal job is to adapt the body to all manner of stress. If you are chilled, the arteries constrict and raise the blood pressure to produce greater warmth. When the bacteria invade the body, the glands provide hormones to produce inflammation which stops infection. In case of severe injury they hasten the clotting of the blood, lower blood pressure to control haemorrhage.

135. How People Themselves Destroy Their Own Happy Life

Jealousy Was The Main Cause of Their Sufferings

Leo Tolstoy the author of two of the world's greatest novels "War and Peace" and "Anna Karenina", married a girl he loved very much. But the girl was very jealous by nature. She used to dress herself up as a peasant and spy on the movements of her husband. She followed him even out in the woods. She became so jealous, even of her own children, that she grabbed a gun and shot a hole in her daughter's photograph. Sometimes she often rolled on the floor with an opium bottle held to her lips and threatened to commit suicide. The children helplessly screamed with terror. None of them realised that they were just squandering their lives. For fifty years they lived in a veritable hell. Neither of them had the sense to say, "Stop! Enough now!" Both of them kept secret diaries in which they blamed each other. The diaries were kept to impress the future generations that the other side was wrong. Before she passed away, she confessed to her daughters: "I was the cause of your father's death". They very well knew she had killed him with her constant complaining, her eternal criticism and her eternal nagging.

Leo Tolstoy's life was a tragedy and the cause of that tragedy was his marriage with a girl who failed to adjust herself according to the circumstances. Her jealousy, suspicion and nagging wrecked the happy home life. This kind of situation is prevailing in many homes in the world due to temperamental differences and their I-ness.

136. How Nagging Wrecked Home Life

Abraham Lincoln's life was also a great tragedy due to his marriage. His wife was always complaining, always criticizing her husband. Lincoln and his wife Marry Todd were opposite in every way: in training, in background, in temperament, in tastes, in mental outlook. They irritated each other constantly when Abraham was just only a lawyer. Her loud shrill voice could be heard across the street, and her incessant outburst of wrath were audible to all who lived near the house. She displayed her anger by other means also. One day in a rage she dashed a cup of hot coffee into her husband's face. She did it in front of many other people. Her jealousy was so foolish, so fierce, so incredible that merely reading about them makes one gasp with astonishment. She finally went insane. It made him regret for his unfortunate marriage, and it made him avoid her presence as much as possible. He often preferred to live in a wretched hotel than his own home to avoid her constant nagging and wild outbursts of temper.

She didn't like the way his huge ears stood out at right angles from his head. She even told him that his nose was't straight, that his lower lip stuck out, that he looked consumptive, that his feet and hands were large, his head too small. She was always complaining and criticising her husband; nothing about him was ever right. He was stoop-shouldered, he walked awkwardly and lifted his feet straight up and down like an Indian. She complained that there was no grace to his movement. Due to her nagging she brought nothing but tragedy into their lives.

We find many such women who have made their own marital graves with a series of little digs.

137. How Suspicion Can Wreck Family Life

Napoleon III of France, nephew of Nepoleon Bonaparte, fell in love with Marie Eugenie Ignace Augustine de Montijo, countess of Teba. She was the most beautiful woman in the world. Her grace, her charm, her youth, her beauty filled him with divine felicity. He married her.

Napoleon and his bride had health, wealth, power, fame, beauty, love, adoration and all the requirements of a perfect romance. But neither the power of his love nor the might of his throne, could keep her from nagging.

Tormented by jealousy, devoured by suspicion, she followed him everywhere and flouted his orders. She denied him even a show of privacy. She broke into his office while he was engaged in affairs of state. She interrupted most important discussions. She refused to leave him alone. She always feared that he might be consorting with another woman. Fed up with that woman Napoleon frequently would steal out by a little side door at night, accompanied by one of the intimate lady who was expecting him.

That is what Eugenie gained from suspicion and nagging. For all the devils in hell for destroying love, suspicion and nagging are the deadliest. Nagging and suspicion are the worst enemies of mankind. No doctor in the world can cure suspicion. Suspicion acts like poison.

This is one of the ways how people due to their foolishness themselves dig their marital graves. They repent only afterwards.

Hatred and suspicion are the deadliest foe of the humanity. These are insatiable like lust and greed. These may temporarily susbside for sometime, and may again burst out with redouble force. If a father dislikes a man, his sons and daughters also begin to hate that man without any rhyme or reason whatsoever, although that man has not done them any wrong or injustice. Such is the force of hatred. If any one even remembers the figure of a man who has done him some serious injury some thirty years ago, at once hatred creeps into his mind and his face shows clear signs of enmity and hatred.

138. Mind is Like a Monkey

In his book "Concentration and Meditation", His Holiness Swami Shiva Nanda says—There is no limit to the power of the human mind. The more concentrated it is, the more power is brought to bear on one point. You are born to concentrate the mind on God after collecting the mental rays that are dissipated on various objects. You forget your duty towards God on account of Moha (attachment) for family, children, money, power, position, name and fame.

Mind is compared to quick-silver, because its rays are scattered over various objects. It is compared to a monkey, because it jumps from one object to another. It is compared to moving air because it is chanchal (Restless).

Concentration is opposed to sensuous desires, bliss to flurry and worry, sustained thinking to perplexity, applied thinking to sloth and torpor, rapture to ill will.

Worldly pleasures intensify the desire for enjoying greater pleasures. Hence the mind of worldlings is very restless. There is no satisfaction and mental peace. Mind can never be satisfied, whatever amount of pleasure you may store up for it.

A scientist concentrates his mind and invents many things. Through concentration he opens the layers of the gross mind and penetrates deeply into higher regions of the mind and gets knowledge. He concentrates all the energies of his mind into one focus and throws them out upon the materials he is analysing and so finds out their secrets.

He who has learnt to manipulate the mind will get the whole Nature under his control.

When you see your dear friend after six years, the happiness that you get is not from the person but from within yourself. The mind becomes concentrated for the time being and you get happiness from within your own self. When the rays of mind are scattered over diverse objects you get pain. When the rays are gathered and collected by practice the mind becomes concentrated and you get happiness from within.

139. Peace

According to His Holiness Swami Shiva Nanda—Peace is a divine attribute. It is a quality of the soul. It cannot remain with a greedy person. It fills the pure heart. It deserts the lustful. It runs away from the lustful. It runs away from the selfish. Wealth, sex, children, prosperity and palatial buildings can not give you everlasting peace. Look within the chambers of your heart. When you are established in the highest self within, you will not be shaken even by heavy sorrow, loss or failure; the inharmonious or disagreeable vibrations. You will tide over all difficulties or crises in life easily and will come out with triumph in all life's experiences. Lead an ideal life of peace.

Kill ruthlessly suspicion, prejudice of all kinds, envy, selfishness, lousy greed of power and possession. Practise daily meditation and establish peace in your mind and heart. Then radiate it to your neighbours and all who come in contact with you. Disseminate it far and wide. Preach the gospel of peace to all men and women of the world. Let go all the worries. Cultivate peace first in the garden of your heart by removing the weeds of lust, hatred, greed, selfishness and jealousy. Wonderful is the power of peace that brings joy and eternal bliss. Peace comes from prayer, Japa, Kirtan, meditation, good and sublime thoughts and understanding.

Do not lose temper when anybody insults, taunts or rebukes you. It is mere play of words and a variety of sounds.

Physical love is animalism. It is passion excited and unrefined. It is gross and sensual. A husband loves his wife, but loves her for the sake of his own self. He is selfish there. He expects sensual pleasure from her. If leprosy or small pox destroys her real beauty, his love for her ceases. Pure love is without selfish attachment. A gross mind with selfishness and lust can not attain peace or spiritual progress.

140. Relaxation

Those who do not know how to relax are comitting slow suicide. Many methods are prescribed for relaxation—Breathing exercises as well as physical measures. In Yoga breathing exercises are called Pranayam. Mr. Hari Dass Chowdhry in his book "Integrated Yoga" has given a number of exercises. In his book "Yoga Asanas", Swami Shiva Nanda has prescribed many such exercises. I am writing here two such exercises.

1. Take your seat in erect posture in a quiet place where there is play of fresh air. Now take in your breath slowly, very slowly, as slowly as you can, until your chest is filled with fresh air. As you are inhaling, think that your whole system is being filled with life and love, or with strength, purity and knowledge. Having deeply taken in the full breath, hold it for a while. Then throw out the breath slowly very slowly, as slowly as you can. At the time of exhaling, your natural tendency might be to throw out the whole breath at once abruptly. But you have to practise a little self control there. While slowly exhaling think that you are eliminating from your system impurity and fatigue. Having completely given out the breath, repeat the process ten to twelve times. Gradually you may increase the number of such rounds of breathing and the duration of practice.

2. Take your seat in erect posture where there is free play of fresh air. Close your right nostril with your finger of right hand and inhale slowly through the left nostril. Feel the air has gone throughout your body. Try to retain the breath for four times of duration of the time in which it was inhaled.

Now close your left nostril with another finger. Now exhale slowly through the right nostril taking twice the time it was inhaled. Now repeat this process in the reverse order, that is by closing the left nostril and inhaling through the right nostril and then closing the right nostril and exhaling through left nostril. You can repeat this process as many times as you like.

If you do not like breathing exercises, then learn to relax through physical measures.

141. Corpse Pose

This is an Asana for relaxation of all muscles, nerves, etc. Spread a soft blanket. Lie flat on your back. Keep the hands on the ground by the sides. Stretch the legs quite straight. Keep the heels close. Let the toes remain separated. Close the eyes. Breathe slowly. Relax all muscles, nerves, organs etc. Start the relaxation process from the toes. Then proceed to the calf-muscles, muscles of the back, chest, arm, forearm and hands, neck, face, etc. See that the abdominal organs, heart, chest, brain are also relaxed. Relax the plexus of nerves also. Do it for a few minutes and repeat this process if you have time. You will enjoy peace, ease, comfort and relaxation. It gives rest not only to the body but also to the mind and soul. It promptly and efficiently ensures complete relaxation and perfect ease. Mind and nerves can't relax while the muscles are tense.

If you are suffering from sleeplessness (Insomnia), then this Asana can help you to go to sleep.

Rest is a must before you get tired. Learn to relax at you work. You can do this exercise sitting in your chair. Ask each muscle turn by turn to relax itself. Say to your muscles to loosen up and relax.

The muscles that are put under severe strain demand relaxation and rest. It is Savasana that promptly and efficiently ensures complete relaxation and perfect ease by the interchange of carbondioxide and oxygen in the tissues.

Rest or sleep taken in the early afternoon after lunch is very useful for relaxing the body and mind.

142. Contentment

Contentment is a positive virtue and not a negative suppression. It is a sublimating force and transforms the desire and greed for transitory objects into a wish to secure universal good and realise God. It gives one a detached outlook towards life and thereby the person develops peace within himself, rising above selfish limitations and avarice. He gets moral strength and his energies will not be dissipated in exerting for petty ends and making himself restless for ordinary gains, aided by jealousy and retaining within hatred towards those better placed.

A contented mind is a continual feast says a maxim. But one may ask, "If I become satisfied with what I have, all my ambitions will die. I may turn lethargic whereas now I am active and energetic". There is, no doubt, truth in this, but by remaining contented, he is sure to divert his efforts to his objects of pursuit with greater efficiency, because he is now endowed with calm and one pointed mind. The gross energy is thus transmuted into a moral force, with which he can try to achieve higher values and ambitions. The mind is restless on account of greed which is often compared to internal fire that consumes a person slowly. Contentment is a powerful antidote to this poison of greed.

In a lecture Swami Vimlanand said, "There are four sentinels who guard the domain of life divine. They are peace, contentment, company of the nobles and discrimination. Anyone who makes friendship with any one of these guards can easily obtain favours from the others. There is no limit to acquire and possess wealth in any form movable or otherwise".

A person's prayers should not be dragged into impure distraction as sensual objects can't provide permanent happiness. Although all people know that contentment is a virtue and provides peace of mind yet they don't try to develop it. This is due to lack of moral strength to enquire into the reality of things.

It is on the strength of contentment that sages live an extremely happy and carefree life. They serve the world in a superior way. Their contentment removed petty mindedness. One of the methods to gain contentment is to engage the mind in constant meditation on God, when the dim of the strife for things mundane will become negligible.

(Reproduced from *The Hindu*)

143. Sayings of The Wise Men On Peace of Mind

1. *Money can buy many things but not peace of mind. It is only you who yourself can find.*
2. *Nothing can bring you peace but your self.*
3. *It is the forgetfulness of the "I-ness" which fills the person with happiness or gives pleasure. To lose oneself is to find oneself.*
4. *The peace of Mind which you hunt outside is hidden within you. All the worries and miseries are the creations of your own mind. By changing your attitude you can easily change them.*
5. *Like a cocoon, you are always weaving threads of thoughts, which keep you imprisoned, involved or enveloped, never allowing a restful moment. Only sleep gives it a little pause.*
6. *Wealth, beauty, name, fame, prosperity, and power, all fail to satisfy man's inner cravings. As a last resort, he turns his attention within and finds there the fountain of happiness.*
7. *A person who can control himself can move the world. Self is that point where the lever of the Archimedes can be placed to lift the world.*
8. *The secret of happiness is hidden in the proper and rightful use of the senses, mind, money and time.*
9. *God has not made anything without any purpose, however tiny, filthy or valueless an object may appear.*
10. *It is not the fault of senses, mind, money or leisure. When we misuse them we encounter difficulties and troubles. These are made to serve you. But their use or misuse is in your own hands.*
11. *Renunciation is from mind. We do not live where our bodies live. We live where our minds live. Solitude can be had at home or it can not be had in remotest forest. (Swami Ram Tirath)*
12. *Money itself is not an enemy. Money is needed at every step. Money can be an excellent aid to progress whether spiritual, mental or material.*

13. *A man does not become an ascetic by merely giving up actions because of laziness, ignorance or hardship of work. An ascetic is one who is endowed with necessary knowledge and practises self discipline and self control.*

14. *According to the Udgith of the Chandogya Upanishad—*
    Earth is the essence of elements,
    Water is the essence of the earth,
    Plants are the essence of water,
    Flowers are the essence of plants,
    Fruits are the essence of flowers,
    Man is the essence of fruits,
    Semen is the seed of the man,
    Speech is the essence of the man.
    Semen is the seed of the man. It is the seed that develops into a tree. Loss of semen results in irritability and anger in temperament. Semen is the source of life. Many insects die after sexual intercourse. One sexual act releases 120 calories of heat, which is equal to the heat produced after running fast for one kilometre or the amount of energy spent in physical labour for ten days, or mental work performed during three days. Excessive loss of semen spreads disease and disaster in the body. Semen is the atomic energy in man. One spermatozoa is capable of producing one human being, while three million are lost at one ejaculation. Use this energy in a judicious manner. Animals and plants are more wise in sexual matters. They do sex only in a particular season. Sex energy can be transmuted for higher creative purposes. Waste of semen is the waste of a vital life force.

15. *Sexual enjoyment is the lowest short lived ecstasy.*

16. *Fighting with the sexual desires dissipate more energy than indulging in sex.*

17. *Pleasure in sex comes from the mind and not from the sexual organs. Sexual organs are only the mediums and not the means.*

165

Those organs obey the commands of the mind. When one realises this, sex stops troubling. Mind should be controlled and disciplined to subdue the superfluous sex desires.

18. Lord Jesus says—If you have lustful look, you have already committed adultery in your heart.

19. Your wife is your companion, co-worker and equal partner in life's struggle. Don't treat her just as an instrument of sexual gratification or as a domestic servant.

20. Very few people march straight to success without going through periods of temporary failures and discouragements. These are the part and parcel of human life.

21. Money can buy many things and can produce wealth. But money can't buy or produce peace of mind. Peace of mind is more valuable than money or wealth.

22. Do as you wish to be done by is the golden rule in human relations.

23. Happiness is contagious in nature. It comes back when you share happiness with others without any selfish motive.

24. Unpeaceful thoughts always make the people sick.

25. Muscle tension is caused due to mental tension. When mental tension is removed, muscle tension also ceases.

26. When we control our emotions we gain power. But when emotions control us the results are often disastrous.

27. To have peace of mind discipline yourself never to get mad or resentful.

28. Don't become a grievance collector. It will surely destroy your own peace of mind.

29. Fatigue is not caused by work or over-work, but by hurry, worry, tension, anxiety and grudges.

30. When you think tiredness you start feeling tired, when you think energy you feel alive. Therefore avoid growing tired in your thoughts and attitude. Keep your eagerness and interest in every aspect of life at a high level. You will start feeling new energy in your body and mind.

31. When you go to sleep don't bother about your plans for the next day.

32. God who has helped you so far, will help you tomorrow also.

33. Worry is a live grave. By avoiding worry we can live longer and better.

34. Fear is one of the main causes of many troubles in the world. Fear often owes its existence to some old vague memory and has no present substance.

35. Your mind can transmute your fear into a real susbstance. When you fear something, that thing is more likely to find you and harm you.

36. If you do not know the method of relaxation, you are slow poisoning your body.

37. Worry, tension, stress, strain and hurry are killing the people like flies.

38. Don't be afraid of criticism. Try to improve yourself in the light of criticism. Go ahead, no matter who criticizes.

39. It is not good to go on searching for symptoms of any imaginary illness. If you will imagine illness, fear illness, you will surely bring illness upon yourself. Mind can transmute your belief into its physical equivalent.

40. Many psychosomatic diseases are caused due to unpeace of mind.

41. Faith has a very strange power of curing even incurable diseases.

42. Nature never takes away anything without replacing with something of equal potential value.

43. Look at your problem in a creative and positive manner and you will find bright opportunities which you have not thought of. Never think negative. Be realistic, face all the facts, but always look on the hopeful side.

44. Before you could win, you had to learn to lose.

45. When you do something helpful for another person you always feel better. It is the secret of happiness.

46. Enthusiasm and eagerness can make any job thrilling. Love

your job. If you do not like it now, learn to like it.

47. Don't take yourself too damn seriously, unless you wish to be damned by others.

48. Lack of money also destroys peace of mind. If you have mastered money you may have peace of mind. If money has mastered you, then you won't have peace of mind. You can be rich with peace of mind. But you can't be rich without peace of mind.

49. Money can buy many things but not peace of mind, but can surely help you to find peace of mind.

50. Nobody who goes too deeply into debt can get peace of mind.

51. The more you give of what you have, the more comes back to you. It is the law of the nature.

52. When you share your blessings with others, you become his creditor. Eventually the debt is paid. Somehow, debts have to be paid.

53. Wealth is not something you grab from others, it is something you build for yourself out of service to others.

54. The motives of love, sex and money rule the world.

55. When you have peace of mind at home you can count on having peace of mind everywhere.

56. Your own mental attitude can make you peaceful or unpeaceful. Control your mental attitude. Negative attitude will lead you towards miseries and positive attitude will lead you towards happiness. A positive mind automatically obtains benefits from other positive minds.

57. A man who works wholeheartedly at his job is not concerned with such matters as finding faults with others.

58. Many successful men do not possess any greater intelligence than most other men possess. Yet their achievements are very high due to their positive mental attitude which makes their brain-power more efficient.

59. Great men have no time to waste with a desire to injure others. If they did, they would not be great men.

60. Fear and anger put the mind behind bars. Guilt wraps the mind in chains.

61. When you befool anybody with clever words, you befool yourself also.
62. One who makes his money through taking dishonest advantage of his fellow men, has cheated himself of the genuine joy which comes with honest success.
63. When you obey the rules of the game, and win, you have done something for your soul. When you cheat and win, you only call it winning. But you have really lost instead.
64. Stress is the cause of many diseases. In this hurry up world we are subjecting ourselves to too many stresses.
65. Learn to live also. You are learning only how to get rich.
66. Never remain angry. Begin each day by liking everyone you meet.
67. Never go to bed angry with your wife.
68. Ill will is also the cause of ill health.
69. Whatever your mind believes can also achieve.
70. Lack of confidence in oneself is one of the greatest barriers to the full expression of your personality.
71. Until you are willing to be your own self at your own level, you can not know yourself, nor know what your mind can accomplish. Nobody can be anyone else without harming his own personality.
72. Peace of mind is the peaceful base upon which we can erect a good deal of life dynamic.
73. A person who is his own master, never seeks revenge on anyone. Revenge can be spuriously sweet, but it is a sweet poison to the personality.
74. A major reason for unhappiness is the tendency to meddle with the lives of others while we take too little time in trying to improve ourselves.
75. If you compromise yourself with your own conscience, you will weaken your conscience. Soon your conscience will fail to guide you, and you never will have real wealth based on peace of mind.
76. Worry is the biggest problem facing mankind. It destroys our ability

to concentrate. When we worry our mind jumps here and there and everywhere. We lose our power of decision making.

77. When we force ourselves to face the worst and accept it mentally, we then eliminate all these vague imaginings and put ourselves in a position in which we are able to concentrate on our problem.

78. According to Dr. Alexis Carrel—"Those who do not know how to fight worry, die young."

79. Most of the patients who come to physicians could cure themselves if they only get rid of their anger, fear, worries, hate, selfishness and their inability to adjust themselves to the world of reality.

80. Many businessmen are wrecking their bodies with heart diseases, ulcers and high blood pressure due to hurry and worry, stress and strain.

81. Always remember even if you are able to acquire the whole world, you could sleep only in one bed at a time and eat only three meals a day, which even an ordinary person can easily do.

82. Nervous troubles are caused by emotions of futility, frustration, anxiety, worry, fear, defeat and despair etc.

83. The main causes of insanity are worry and fear.

84. According to Alexis Carrel—"Those who keep the peace of their inner selves in the midst of the tumult of the modern city are immune to nervous diseases".

85. According to the American Dental Association—"Unpleasant emotions such as those caused by worry, fear and nagging. . . may upset the body's calcium balance and cause tooth decay."

86. According to William James—"The Lord may forgive our sins, but the nervous system never does."

87. A cheerful mental attitude helps the body to fight diseases.

88. Many worries are caused due to making decisions before they have sufficient knowledge on which to base decision.

89. Trivialities are at the bottom of most of our marital unhappiness. We allow ourselves to be upset by small things we should despise and forget.

90. *Nearly all of our worries and unhappiness come from our imagination and not from reality. We worry about things that rarely happen.*

91. *Don't worry about those things which are beyond your power and leave them to the will of God. It is useless to fight with the inevitable.*

92. *According to Marcus Aurelius—"Our life is what our thoughts make it." Happy thoughts make us happy and miserable thoughts make us miserable.*

93. *When we hate our enemies, we are giving them power over our sleep, our appetite. Hatred destroys our ability to enjoy even our food. It increases our Blood Pressure and affects our health and happiness.*

94. *If you have a weak heart, then even one fit of anger can kill you.*

95. *If you can't love your enemies, then atleast forgive them and forget them for the sake of your own health.*

96. *According to Epictetus—"Every man will pay the penalty for his own misdeeds. The man who remembers this will be angry with no one, indignant with no one, revile no one, offend no one and hate no one".*

97. *According to Lincoln—"All of us are the children of conditions, of circumstances, of environment, of education, of acquired habits and of heredity moulding men as they are and will forever be.*

98. *It is natural to forget to be grateful. So, it is folly to expect gratitude for any of our work. If you want to enjoy happiness, stop thinking about gratitude or ingratitude. Do work only for the inner joy of giving.*

99. *Those who do not teach their children to express gratitude, they should not expect gratitude from them. To raise grateful children, we have to be grateful ourselves. Don't belittle the kindness of others in the presence of your children.*

100. *Most of the things in our lives are right and only a few are wrong. To keep oneself happy try to concentrate on right things*

and avoid wrong things. But if you want unhappiness then concentrate on wrong things and avoid right things.

101. *Think of all we have to be grateful for and thank God for all our boons and bounties.*

102. *According to Jonathan Swift, author of Gulliver's Travels— "The best doctors in the world are—Doctor Diet, Doctor Quiet, and Doctor Merryman".*

103. *Never do anything you don't like yourself.*

104. *According to Prophet Mohammed—"Do a good deed every-day. A good deed is one that brings a smile of joy to the face of another."*
   When we try to please others, it causes us to stop thinking about ourselves. And this saves us from worry, fear and melancholy.

105. *Religious life helps us to protect ourselves from ulcer, angina pectoris, nervous breakdown, and insanity.*

106. *According to Dr. Carrel—"Prayer is the most powerful form of energy one can generate. When we pray, we link ourselves with the inexhaustible motive power that spins the universe. Whenever we address God in fervent prayer, we change both soul and body for the better. It helps us to put into words exactly what is troubling us and gives us relief."*

107. *In every person there are deep wells of hidden strength that are never found and used. Yogis awaken their Kundalini to arouse that sleeping power and utilize that power for spiritual progress.*

108. *Vulgar people always feel happy when they criticize others. Don't bother about your unjust criticism. It may prove a blessing in disguise for you.*

109. *Most of our fatigue is caused due to our mental and emotional attitude. Boredom, resentment, a feeling of not being appreciated, a feeling of futility, hurry, worry and anxiety like emotional factors cause fatigue.*

110. *If you don't find happiness in your work, you may never find it anywhere. Getting interested in your job will take your mind off your worries.*

111. *No one ever died due to lack of sleep. Nature itself takes care of your necessary sleep. Worrying about insomnia causes more damage than sleeplessness itself.*

112. *Those who don't know how to relax their bodies and minds are committing slow suicide.*

113. *Many divorces are caused due to lack of proper sexual knowledge by either of the partners. It would be better to read any good book on sex to avoid sex related troubles.*

114. *Everybody wants appreciation and recognition. They are ready to do anything to get it.*

115. *Accumulation mania is at the opposite pole from a mind that knows peace. Rich men are always filled with hatred and mistrust. Their worst hatred is directed towards the Government. They prophecy that the Government could cause them to die as a pauper.*

116. *Rest or sleep taken in the early afternoon (siesta) after lunch provides relaxation to body and mind.*

144. Your Passport To Peace of Mind

This book is like your passport to reach at the destination where Peace of Mind resides. After reading this book, now your mind can easily understand—What is peace of mind? How can one attain peace of mind? Who are the enemies of Peace? What is/was troubling your mind? How were you harming your nervous system and your heart by useless anger, hate, greed, envy, jealousy, ill will, hurry, worry, stress and strain etc.? You were unnecessarily losing your temper over useless trifles.

PEACE OF MIND MISSION can help you if you have any problem about your peace of mind. You just write us a letter stating your problem in detail. Ours is a Voluntary Organisation. We will try to find a solution of your problem. Half of your problem will automatically be solved when you write it in detail. Most of the people never think about peace of mind. When you start thinking about Peace of mind, you start moving towards peace of mind. You must write stating—

1. What is your problem?

2. What steps have you taken so far to solve that problem?

3. What is the result of your efforts?

4. What are your expectations?

5. What is your profession?

Write to—
Hari Datt Sharma,
PEACE OF MIND MISSION,
3152/6, Gali No. 9,
Ranjit Nagar, (South Patel Nagar),
New Delhi—110008.
Phone : 5711650